SAINT JOHN PAUL II
AND THE LAITY

SAINT JOHN PAUL II
AND THE LAITY

The Pope's Teachings on the Call, Theology, Spirituality, and Ministry of Laity

Leonard Doohan

WIPF & STOCK · Eugene, Oregon

Wipf and Stock Publishers
199 W 8th Ave, Suite 3
Eugene, OR 97401

Saint John Paul II and the Laity
The Pope's Teachings on the Call, Theology, Spirituality, and Ministry of Laity
By Doohan, Leonard
Copyright©1984 by Doohan, Leonard
ISBN 13: 978-1-5326-1520-7
Publication date 12/5/2016
Previously published by Le Jacq Publishing Inc, 1984

CONTENTS

PREFACE

Since his elevation to the See of Peter, Pope John Paul II has created for himself more encounters with the laity of the world than any other pope in the history of Christianity. He has traveled extensively throughout the world and both listened to and spoken with laity of all walks of life. He has visited their churches, factories, civic centers, and national government offices. He has shared their joy in their weddings, pride in their culture, satisfaction in their work.

Although the Church has had a series of excellent popes since the turn of the century, John Paul II stands out as the one great religious leader who has himself been immersed in the daily grind and joys of lay life. He knows the hardships of the factory, the exhilaration of sport, the intellectual challenge of university life, and the daily pressures of unjust government. In his many journeys of recent years, we have seen him at home with church leaders, politicians, workers, and youth. He has chosen to address the laity of the world on a broad spectrum of topics, and it is truly exciting to read his reflections.

The pages that follow contain some of the Pope's insights into the nature of lay life and a selection of his challenges to laity today. Punctuation, spelling, and capitalization have been made consistent throughout the work to eliminate differences among translations and to increase readability. Where necessary, I have carefully adapted nouns, pronouns, and adjectives to eliminate sexist language from the translation of the generic original, while maintaining the meaning of the original passage.

Numbers in parentheses appearing throughout the text refer to a list of John Paul II's speeches, with bibliographic information, located at the back of the book.

The work makes no claim to be complete. After an attentive reading of most of the Pope's speeches made during his early years in Rome, selections were drawn from about three hundred of his sermons and addresses. I hope that the work gives readers a glimpse into the mind, heart, and vision of Pope John Paul II, regarding the present and future life and role of laity in the Church, and that his thoughts and reflections inspire us all in our daily living of the Lord's call.

Acknowledgement is gratefully given to the editor of *L'Osservatore Romano* for permission to use material from the English edition; and to the Director and Editor-in-Chief of National Catholic News Service for permission to use material from *Origins*.

CHAPTER I

DEFINITIONS OF THE LAY PERSON

Disciples and followers of Christ.

Called to sanctity, discipleship, and fidelity; endowed with the common priesthood, Christ's threefold mission, and a Catholic identity; made sharers in spiritual worship, evangelization, ecclesial responsibility, discernment, and a partnership with the Pope; committed to the apostolate, ongoing education, optimism, and the integration of faith and life; baptised into the Church as a community, a pilgrim people, a sacrament of salvation, and a herald of faith.

A leaven in the reality of the world.

The laity's special dignity and mission: participants in the entire reality of the world, witnesses to a new humanity, transformers of the world, leaven of world developments, an ecclesial presence to the world in an individual or organized apostolate.

All have a vocation and responsibility of their own.

Called for a mission of salvation, given a mandate of salvation in the ordinary circumstances of life. Everyone's vocation is a mystery of God, calling each one to decide for Christ and leading to personal fulfillment.

Each one has a place in this building up of the Body of Christ.

John Paul II reminds everyone of their personal and unique call: the handicapped, artisans, athletes, researchers, newlyweds, elderly, prisoners, teachers, youth, domestic workers, the sick.

Disciples and Followers of Christ

Called to sanctity, discipleship, and fidelity. The Christian vocation is sublime and demanding, and it would be unrealizable for us if the Spirit of God did not give us the light to understand and the strength necessary to act. But Christ has also assured us of his assistance: "Behold I am with you all days, even to the end of the world" (Mt 28:20). Yes, the Christian vocation is a vocation to perfection in order to build up the Body of Christ "until we become one in faith and in the knowledge of God's Son, and form that perfect man who is Christ come to full stature" (Eph 4:13). Firm in the faith, may we be able to grow in every way "practicing the truth in charity" (Eph 4:15). (135, p. 423)

This reminds us that the laity are by definition disciples and followers of Christ, members of the Church who are present and active in the world's heart so as to administer temporal realities and order them toward God's reign. (170, p. 135)

Finally, insofar as the faithful are concerned—as the word itself signifies—fidelity of its very nature must be a duty in keeping with their condition as Christians. They show it with ready and sincere hearts and give proof of it either by obeying the sacred pastors whom the Holy Spirit has placed to rule the Church of God (cf. Acts 20:28) or by collaborating in those plans and works for which they have been called. (1, pp. 3–4)

Endowed with the common priesthood, Christ's threefold mission, a Catholic identity. You know that the doctrine of the common priesthood of the faithful offers the laity a providential occasion for ever-further discovery of the vocation of every baptized person to the apostolate and necessary, active, and conscious commitment to the Church's task. The doctrine of the common priesthood of the faithful was amply developed by the Council. It gives rise to a vast and consoling flowering of initiatives and works. These constitute an invaluable contribution for announcement of the Christian message, both in mission lands and in countries, such as yours, where the necessity of supplementing the priest's presence with the aid of the laity is more acutely felt. This is consoling. We ought first to rejoice at this collaboration from the laity and to encourage it. (165, p. 143)

He who was born of the Virgin Mary, the carpenter's son (as he was thought to be), the Son of the living God (confessed by Peter), came to make us all "a Kingdom of priests." The Second Vatican Council has reminded us of the mystery of this power and of the fact that Christ's mission as priest, prophet-teacher, and king continues in the Church. Everyone, the whole people of God, shares in this threefold mission. . . . All "sacred power" exercised in the Church is nothing other than service, service with a single purpose: to ensure that all the people of God share in this threefold mission of Christ and always remain under the power of the Lord, power that has its source not in the powers of this world but in the mystery of the cross and resurrection. (4, p. 307)

This coherence implies an awareness of your identity as Catholics; it means giving public witness to it. The Church today needs lay people who will give witness to their faith and share her mission in the world, being the ferment of faith, justice, and human dignity, in order to build a more human and fraternal world from which we can look up to God.

The pope expects from you a loyal acceptance of the Church. You cannot be faithful and remain attached to secondary things, valid in the past but already outdated. You will not be faithful either if you try to build the so-called church of the future, unrelated to the present (50, p. 542)

Made sharers in spiritual worship, evangelization, ecclesial responsibility, discernment, and a partnership with the pope. Let us give thanks today for this gift of our baptism: by making us participate in the life of God, it makes us participate in the spiritual worship of Christ, in his prophetic mission, in his royal service, which constitute the priesthood common to all the baptized, "Recognize, O Christian, your dignity!" (205, p. 1)

As members of the laity, you are called to take an active part in the sacramental and liturgical life of the Church, especially in the eucharistic sacrifice. At the same time you are called to spread the gospel actively through the practice of charity and through involvement in catechetical and missionary efforts, according to the gifts that each one of you has received (cf. 1 Cor 12:4ff). In every Christian community, whether it be the "domestic church" constituted by the family or the parish collaborating with the priest, or the diocese united around the bishop, the laity strive, like the followers of Christ in the first century, to remain faithful to the teaching of the apostles, faithful to fraternal service, and faithful to prayer and to the celebration of the Eucharist (cf. Acts 2:42). (155, p. 48)

We must, however, always keep in mind the truth that every initiative is based on adequate awareness of the individual Christian's vocation and of responsibility for this singular, unique, and unrepeatable grace by which each Christian in the community of the people of God builds up the body of Christ. . . . It is the basis on which their lives must be built by married people, parents, and women and men of different conditions and professions, from those who occupy the highest posts in society to those who perform the simplest tasks. It is precisely the principle of the "kingly service" that imposes on all of us, in imitation of Christ's example, the duty to demand of ourselves exactly what we have been called to, what we have personally obliged ourselves to by God's grace, in order to respond to our vocation. (73, p. 641)

The Church, therefore, does not accomplish this discernment only through the pastors, who teach in the name and with the power of Christ, but also through the laity: Christ "made them his witnesses and gave them understanding of faith and the grace of speech (cf. Acts 2:17–18; Rv 19:10) so that the power of the gospel might shine forth in their daily social and family life." The laity, moreover, by reason of their particular vocation, have the specific role of interpreting the history of the world in the light of Christ, inasmuch as they are called to illuminate and organize temporal realities according to the plan of God, creator and redeemer. (250, p. 440)

By baptism and confirmation you are called by him to share in the mission of his Church—in his own mission of salvation. And the Pope is deeply grateful for all that you are doing to advance God's Kingdom of truth and life, of holiness and grace, of justice, love, and peace. He is thrilled to have your partnership in the gospel of Christ. (6, p. 4)

Committed to the apostolate, ongoing education, optimism, and the integration of faith and life. The necessity of the lay apostolate is derived from this and is defined as a due response to the gifts received. In this connection, I think it will be well to take up again—I confine myself to a mere mention of it—that conciliar text that on the biblical and theological foundations of our insertion through the baptism in the Mystical Body of Christ and through the power received from the Spirit by means of confirmation presents the ministry that appertains to each member of the Church as a "noble obligation of working."

"For the exercise of the apostolate—it is added—he (the Holy Spirit) gives the faithful special gifts," from which is derived correlatively the obligation of operating and cooperating "for the building up of the whole body in charity" (cf. Decree Apostolicam Actuositatem, introduction and no. 3). (157, p. 16)

"The Church, as regards her specific mission, must promote and impart Christian education, to which all the baptized are entitled so that they may reach the maturity of faith. As the servant of all people, the Church tries to collaborate through her members, especially laity, in tasks of human cultural advancement in all forms that interest society." (Medellin Conference, 1968, Education, no. 9)

Prepare for life with seriousness and diligence. At this moment of youth, so important for the full maturing of your personality, always give an adequate place to the religious element in your formation, the one that brings all to attainment of their full dignity, which is that of being children of God. Always remember that only if one builds, as St. Paul says, on the one foundation that is Jesus Christ (cf. 1 Cor 3:11) will one be able to construct something really great and lasting.

As a memory of this meeting so cordial and joyful, I wish to leave you a concrete consideration. With the vivacity that is characteristic of your age, with the generous enthusiasm of your young hearts, walk toward Christ. He alone is the solution to all your problems. He alone is the way, the truth, and the life: he alone is the real salvation of the world: he alone is the hope of humankind.

Seek Jesus: endeavor to acquire a deep personal faith that will inform and direct your whole life. But above all, let it be your commitment and your program to love Jesus, with a sincere, authentic, and personal love. He must be your friend and your support along the path of life. He alone has words of eternal life (cf. Jn 6:68).

Your thirst for the absolute cannot be quenched with ideological substitutes that lead to hatred, violence, and despair. Christ alone, sought and loved with sincere love, is a source of joy, serenity, and peace.

But after having met Christ, after having discovered who he is, you cannot fail to feel the necessity of proclaiming him. Be real witnesses of Christ; live and proclaim your faith with deeds and with words. (57, p. 8)

The most subtle temptation that today afflicts Christians, and the young in particular, is precisely that of renunciation of hope in the victory of Christ. The prompter of every snare, the Evil One, has always striven to extinguish the light of this hope in the heart of every person. Christian struggle is not an easy way, but we must follow it, aware that we possess an inner force of transformation, communicated to us with the divine life that has been bestowed on us in Christ the Lord. By virtue of your witness, you will make it understood that the highest human values are undertaken in a Christianity lived consistently, and that the faith of the gospel does not just propose a new vision of humanity and the universe, but bestows above all the capacity of bringing about this renewal.

In this connection, I recall to you the words addressed to the young by the Council Fathers at the conclusion of the Ecumenical Council: "The Church looks to you with confidence and with love. . . . She possesses what constitutes the strength and the charm of youth, that is to say, the ability to rejoice with what is beginning, to give oneself and to set out again for new conquests."

Without certain hope in Christ's victory in you and in the world that surrounds you, there can be no optimism; and without optimism, that serene gaiety that is characteristic of the young cannot exist. There are still too many young people today who have already renounced youth. (99, p. 3)

The Second Vatican Council teaches the doctrine on the mission of the whole People of God, which has been called to take part in the mission of Christ himself (cf. Dogmatic Constitution *Lumen Gentium,* nos. 10–12). It is a triple mission. Christ—Priest, Prophet, and King—expressed his mission to the end in the paschal mystery, in the Resurrection.

Each of us in this large community of the Church, of the People of God, takes part in this mission by means of the sacrament of baptism. Each of us is called to faith in the Resurrection like Thomas: "Put your finger here, and see my hands; and put out your hand, and place it in my side; do not be faithless, but believing" (Jn 20:27).

All of us have the duty of defining the meaning of our own life by means of this faith. This life has a very varied form. It is we ourselves who give it a determined form. And it is precisely our faith that brings it about that the life of each one of us is penetrated somewhere by this mission, which Jesus Christ, our Redeemer, accepted from the Father and shared with us. Faith brings it about that some part of the paschal mystery penetrates the life of each of us. A certain irradiation of it.

We must find this ray in order to live in it every day for all this time, which began again on the Day that the Lord has made. (95, p. 11)

Baptized into the Church as a community, a pilgrim people, a sacrament of salvation, and a herald of faith. God who calls all people to his service and assigns a task to each one has a fundamental right to do so. He alone has this right, because he is the Creator and Redeemer of each of us. If he calls us, if he invites us to follow a given way, he does so in order that we will not dissipate his work; in order that we may respond with our own lives to the gift received from him; in order that we may live in a way worthy of the human being, who is "a temple of God;" in order that we may be able to carry out that particular duty, which he wishes to entrust to us. . . .

A life of faith, which has its beginning in the family, dynamically integrated in the parish, and which develops from baptism to the meeting with Christ in death: following the principle of the close collaboration between the family and the parish, which cooperate together in the formation of the responsible and mature Christian.

Here, therefore, is the indispensable necessity of parish catechesis, which integrates and completes the teaching of religion imparted at school and connects religious knowledge with sacramental life. . . .

I would like this moving and generous readiness to accept God's call to be always present in all the many faithful of this parish, to form a living Christian community, joyful and proud to be able to say "yes" to Christ and to the Church. (41, p. 3)

At a time when the whole church has become newly aware of being the people of God, a people sharing in the mission of Christ, a people that goes through history with that mission, a "pilgrim" people . . . human beings are incapable of understanding themselves fully without Christ. They cannot understand who they are, nor what their true dignity is, nor what their vocation is, nor what their final end is. They cannot understand any of this without Christ. (102, p. 56)

Through her continual evangelizing presence, the Church, a "sacrament of salvation," does nothing but carry out her mission of service for all people, in order to make the kingdom of God present among them. This kingdom is not only one of peace, justice, and love. Hence her constant and self-sacrificing solicitude to revive also in consciences the concern to perfect this land, where the human family grows (cf. Constitution *Gaudium et Spes*, no. 39). Such beloved goods as human dignity, freedom, excellent fruits of human nature and enterprise, are spread on earth in the Spirit of the Lord and in accordance with his command. (23, p. 7)

A word of greeting and exhortation addressed expressly to the lay people; to those, above all, who with generous availability, take their place at the side of their pastors in order to assume the responsibility for evangelization with them. (79, p. 6)

My fraternal encouragement goes likewise in your endeavors to promote the participation of the laity in the Church's mission of salvation. I am confident that a realization by the laity of their distinctive and indispensible role will bear ever greater fruits in the years to come. At the same time, may the laity be ever more aware of their sacramental configuration to Jesus Christ and of their personal vocation to holiness within the community of an evangelizing and catechizing Church. (194, pp. 3, 12)

It is important that we too, Christians set by Providence to live in the conclusive years of this second millenium, should revive deep awareness of the mysterious ways through which it carries out the plan of salvation. God communicated himself irrevocably in Christ. It is by means of the Spirit, however, that the Risen Christ lives and acts permanently in our midst and can make himself present in every "here" and "now" of human experience in history.

With deep joy and fervent gratitude we renew, therefore, our act of faith in Christ, the Redeemer, well aware that "no one can say 'Jesus is Lord' except by the Holy Spirit" (1 Cor 12:3). It is he who unites us in a single body in the unity of the Christian vocation and in the multiplicity of charisms. It is he who carries out the sanctification and unity of the Church (cf. *Roman Pontifical,* "Rite of Confirmation," nos. 24, 47). (193, p. 11)

A Leaven in the Reality of the World

The laity's special dignity and mission. Today I would like to speak to you about that special dignity and mission entrusted to the lay people in the Church. St. Peter says that Christians are "a royal priesthood, a holy nation" (1 Pt 2:9). All Christians, incorporated into Christ and his Church by baptism, are consecrated to God. They are called to profess the faith that they have received. By the sacrament of confirmation, they are further endowed by the Holy Spirit with special strength to be witnesses of Christ and sharers in his mission of salvation. Every lay Christian is therefore an extraordinary work of God's grace and is called to the heights of holiness.

Sometimes lay men and women do not seem to appreciate to the full the dignity and the vocation that are theirs as lay people. No, there is no such thing as an "ordinary lay person," for all of you have been called to conversion through the death and resurrection of Jesus Christ. As God's holy people you are called to fulfill your role in the evangelization of the world.

Yes, the laity are "a chosen race, a holy priesthood," also called to be "the salt of the earth" and "the light of the world."

It is their specific vocation and mission to express the gospel in their lives and thereby to insert the gospel as a leaven into the reality of the world in which they live and work. The great forces that shape the world—politics, the mass media, science, technology, culture, education, industry and work—are precisely the areas where lay people are especially competent to exercise their mission. If these forces are guided by people who are true disciples of Christ and who are, at the same time, fully competent in the relevant secular knowledge and skill, then indeed will the world be transformed from within by Christ's redeeming power. (119, p. 324)

You know very well how the Second Vatican Council took up this great contemporary historical movement of the "advancement of the laity," studying it in its theological foundations, integrating it, and illuminating it completely in the ecclesiology of *Lumen Gentium,* convoking and giving impetus to the active participation of laity in the life and mission of the Church. In the Body of Christ constituted in "plurality of ministries but unity of mission" (Decree *Apostolicam Actuositatem,* no. 2; cf. Dogmatic Constitution *Lumen Gentium,* nos. 10, 32), laity as Christian faithful "are by baptism made one body, with Christ, and are established among the People of God. They are in their own way made sharers in the priestly, prophetic, and kingly functions of Christ." They are called to exercise their apostolate, in particular, "in each and in all of the secular professions and occupations" that they carry out and "in the ordinary circumstances of family and social life" (Dogmatic Constitution *Lumen Gentium,* no. 31), in order to "penetrate and perfect the temporal sphere with the spirit of the gospel" (Decree *Apostolicam Actuositatem,* no. 5).

In the overall framework of the conciliar teachings and especially in the light of the "Constitution on the Church," vast requirements and renewed prospects of lay action were opened in very varied fields of ecclesial and secular life.

Among the vast expanse of the fields that call for the presence of the laity in the world, and which are pointed out by the Apostolic Exhortation *Evangelii Nuntiandi*—this magna charta of evangelization—I wish to mention some fundamental and urgent spaces in the accelerated and unequal process of industrialization, urbanization, and cultural transformation in the lives of our peoples.

The safeguarding, advancement, sanctification, and apostolic projection of family life must count Catholic laity among their most decisive and consistent agents. (54, p. 6)

Participants in the entire reality of the world. Actually, all the faithful by virtue of their baptism and of the sacrament of confirmation must profess publicly the faith received from God by means of the Church, spread it and defend it as true witnesses of Christ (cf. Dogmatic Constitution *Lumen Gentium,* no. 11). That is, they are called to evangelization, which is a fundamental duty of all the members of the people of God (cf. *Ad Gentes,* no. 55), whether or not they have special functions more closely connected with the duties of pastors (Decree *Apostolicam Actuositatem,* no. 24).

In fact, the laity, who by divine vocation participate in the entire reality of the world, instilling into it their faith, which has become a reality in their own public and private life (cf. Jas 2:17), are the most immediate protagonists of the renewal of human beings and of things. With their active presence as believers, they work at the progressive consecration of the world to God (cf. Dogmatic Constitution *Lumen Gentium*, no. 34). This presence is linked with the whole economy of the Christian religion, which is, indeed, a doctrine, but is above all an event; the event of the Incarnation, Jesus, the God-man who recapitulated in himself the universe (cf. Eph 1:10). . . .

The apostolate of the laity, understood and put into practice, in this way, gives to all the events of human history their full meaning, respecting their autonomy and encouraging the progress required by the very nature of each of them. At the same time, it gives us the key to interpret fully the meaning of history, since all temporal realities, like the events that manifest them, take on their deepest meaning in the spiritual dimension that establishes the relationship between the present and the future (cf. Heb 13:14). Disregard or mutilation of this dimension would become, in fact, an attack on the very essence of the human being. (56, p. 9)

Is it not the laity who are called, by reason of their vocation in the Church, to make their contribution in the political and economic dimensions and to be effectively present in the safeguarding and advancement of human rights? (51, p. 538)

Witnesses to a new humanity. At the heart of the situations and problems on which humanity's future depends, the laity must, in particular, be the witness of a new humanity, create new spaces in which community may be experienced, nourish its creative imagination on the dynamism of the gospel, and set the example of the generous sacrifice—involving the difficult balance between prudence and courage—of those who struggle to open to Christ, the Lord of history, the doors of each person's heart. . . .

Among the vast fields of action of the Christian laity, your Assembly has selected three fundamental ones: the family, work, and culture. . . .

The family, work, and culture are three essential centers around which human beings' lives are woven, their humanity is realized, and their Christian personality as children of God, brothers and sisters of their fellow human beings, and masters of creation is constructed. They are universal aspects, determinant for complete human development and for the original contribution of the gospel to social life; they are aspects that represent a challenge. (240, p. 4)

Transformers of the world. You who are lay persons in the Church and who possess faith, the greatest of all resources—you have a unique opportunity and crucial responsibility. Through your lives in the midst of your daily activities in the world, you show the power that faith has to transform the world and to renew the family of humanity. Even though it is hidden and unnoticed like the leaven or the salt of the earth spoken of in the gospel, your role as laity is indispensable for the Church in the fulfillment of her mission from Christ. This was clearly taught by the fathers of the Second Vatican Council, when they stated: "The Church is not truly established and does not fully live, nor is she a perfect sign of Christ among people, unless there exists a laity worthy of the name, working alongside the hierarchy. For the gospel cannot be deeply imprinted on the mentality, life, and work of any people without the active presence of lay people" (*Ad Gentes*, no. 21).

The role of lay people in the mission of the Church extends in two directions: in union with your pastors and assisted by their guidance you build up the communion of the faithful; second, as responsible citizens you permeate with the leaven of the gospel the society in which you live, in its economic, social, political, cultural, and intellectual dimension. (155, p. 47)

The culture you profess must, furthermore, recognize and live God's transcendency over human beings; that is, it must be animated by a Christian inspiration. This is the task that the Council entrusts to you: "it belongs to the laity to seek the kingdom of God by engaging in temporal affairs and directing them according to God's will" (Dogmatic Constitution *Lumen Gentium*, no. 31). When temporal things are not directed to God, sooner or later they are even referred to human beings but come into opposition with him. Your professionality, like that of every Christian professional, will therefore have to be imbued also with an interior inspiration, coming from Christian spirituality. The Christian spirit will have to guide every lay person, and especially those who have received the task of research and cultural discernment, to penetrate, actualize, and develop all the values that the gospel has spread in history, to continue "to put to use"—as my venerated predecessor Paul VI wrote in the Apostolic Exhortation *Evangelii Nuntiandi*—"every Christian and evangelical possibility latent but already present and active in the affairs of the world" (no. 70).

Faithful to the cultural and spiritual requirements of your professions, you can put into practice that "maturation of civil conscience in the evangelical spirit," to which the statutory premise of your Regulation and your history call you (no. 2) and operate with consistency in all circumstances "to unite all things in him, things in heaven and things on earth" (Constitution *Gaudium et Spes*, no. 45), that is, in morals and in laws, which regard particularly human beings in their fundamental rights and values, according to the teachings of the ecclesiastical Magisterium. (161, p. 16)

Leaven of world development. That lay people have a specific duty in this field, I have had occasion to stress repeatedly, in close harmony, furthermore, with the directions given by the Council. "As God's holy people," I said, for example, at Limerick, in the course of my pilgrimage in Ireland, "you are called to fulfill your role in the evangelization of the world. Yes, the laity are 'a chosen race, a holy priesthood,' also called to be 'the salt of the earth' and 'the light of the world.' It is their specific vocation and mission to express the gospel in their lives and thereby to insert the gospel as a leaven into the reality of the world in which they live and work. The great forces that shape the world— politics, the mass media, science, technology, culture, education, industry, and work—are precisely the areas where lay people are especially competent to exercise their mission. If these forces are guided by people who are true disciples of Christ, and who are at the same time fully competent in the relevant secular knowledge and skill, then indeed will the world be transformed from within by Christ's redeeming power." (176, p. 4)

An ecclesial presence to the world. In the first place, is it necessary to repeat to you how much the Church—and the Pope in her name— counts on your apostolate as laity? The work that falls specifically to you in the Church is essential. No one can replace you, neither priests nor sisters, whom I do not fail, as you know, to encourage in their specific role. Preachers and educators in the faith, the priests are there to help you to impregnate your lives with the spirit of the gospel and to unite the spiritual offering of your lives with that of Christ. Their role is indispensable, and you must be greatly concerned, you too, about priestly vocations. Likewise, men and women religious are there to bear witness to the beatitudes and to undivided love of Christ. I ask them to act as priests, as religious, and you must act as real laity, responsible day in and day out for the family, social, and professional tasks in which you incarnate the presence and the witness of Christ, in which you try to make this world and its structures a world more worthy of the children of God.

In this way you develop, as Christians, all your capacities as men, and likewise women, who have a magnificent role to play in the apostolate today, with all the resources of their femininity, in a world in which they have and take their place and accept their responsibilities to an ever increasing extent. In short, you all take part in the mission of the Church, in its prophetic, priestly, and royal mission, by virtue of your baptism and your confirmation.

Happy Vatican II, which highlighted your "vocation as laity," linking it up with the life of the people of God as a whole! There is no need for me to mention to you the constitution *Lumen Gentium* (nos. 30–38) or the decree *Apostolicam Actuositatem,* which must remain the charter of your rights and duties in the Church. (159, p. 5)

In an individual or organized apostolate. The Second Vatican Council presented the greatness of the vocation of the laity, who by their presence and activity in the order of temporal things must be living witnesses to the faith. It also showed that this witness can be an individual and personal apostolate, but it clearly pointed out the conditions of organized apostolate, which correspond to the social nature of human beings, and specified apostolate of the hierarchy (*Christus Dominus,* no. 33).

As regards Catholic Action more concretely, beyond activities of exclusively temporal character or of mere social assistance, it brings its members deep awareness of their apostolic vocation in their own situation as lay people. As the Second Vatican Council rightly teaches: "The Church is not truly established and does not fully live nor is a perfect sign of Christ unless there is a genuine laity existing and working alongside the hierarchy" (*Ad Gentes,* no. 21). (115, p. 12)

For you lay people, this apostolic life calls for effective openness to your various environments in order to cause the evangelical "leaven" to penetrate them. It involves multiple activities and responsibilities to be assumed in all areas of human life: the family, professions, society, culture, and politics. It is by assuming these responsibilities competently and in deep union with God that you will fulfill your vocation as laity and Christians: that you will sanctify yourselves and sanctify the world.

To remain united with God in the accomplishment of the tasks incumbent upon you is a vital necessity to bear witness to his Love. Only a sacramental life and a life of prayer will be able to cause this intimacy with the Lord to grow.

To take time to pray and to nourish prayer and activities through biblical, theological, and doctrinal study; to live by Christ and his grace by receiving assiduously the sacraments of reconciliation and the Eucharist, such are the fundamental requirements of every deeply Christian life. Thus the Holy Spirit will be the source both of your action and of your contemplation, which will then interpenetrate each other, support each other, and yield abundant fruit.

This deep unity between prayer and action is at the basis of all spiritual renewal, especially among the laity. It is at the basis of the great enterprises of evangelization and construction of the world according to God's plan. It must underlie the life of your movements and their means of formation in view of evangelization.

It must also be lived in the Church, for it does not concern individuals or isolated movements, whose spiritual and doctrinal autonomy can lead only to sectarianism and frustration. On the contrary, it is an expression of the union of Christ and the Church.

That is why it is necessary not to lose sight of the fact that each of your movements is a living cell of the Church and that all members, to carry out their function, must be attached to the Body of Christ and need one another (cf. 1 Cor 12:12–27). Your inspirations, your aims, are different but complementary. No movement can exclude others, be self-sufficient, or represent the only way of renewal, without running the risk of losing its sap, drying up, and failing in its mission. (146, p. 5)

All Have a Vocation and Responsibility of Their Own

Called for a mission of salvation. Each one of you is individually called by Christ, called to be part of his Kingdom and to play a role in his mission of salvation. These are the great realities of your Confirmation. Having called you by name, God sends you forth to accomplish what he wants you to do. He says to each of you what he said to Jeremiah the Prophet: "I am with you to protect you." He seals his protection over you by putting his words into your mouth. In the expression of the Psalmist, the word of God becomes for you a lamp for your feet and a light for your path (cf. Ps 119:105). Christ calls you to lead a new life based on the Beatitudes, with new criteria of judgment, a fresh spiritual outlook, and a transformed pattern of life. Incorporated into the newness of Christ's own life, only a constant turning to him will give you fulfillment and joy. A repeated conversion of heart becomes the condition for the usefulness of your activities and for the attainment of your destiny.

As you pursue your fundamental Christian calling, you will be summoned to perform joyfully and faithfully the activities of each moment, each day, each week. For most of you, the field of your activities is the secular world itself in need of the gospel leaven. Your task is crystal clear: to bring Christ to the world and to bring the world to Christ. I am sure that you have already grasped all of this. Is this not the context of your motto: "To do more, to love more, to serve more"?

This "doing," this "loving," this "serving" must be expressed in many ways. You are called, for instance, to be men and women of honesty and integrity: "to live in truth and love" according to the petition of this morning's Mass. You are called to open your hearts to the justice of the gospel, so that in turn you may be instruments of justice and builders of peace.

You are young, and you are rightfully looking for understanding from your elders, your priests, your beloved parents, who make up the preceding generations of society—and you are hoping for the compassion of friendship. But precisely because you are young, with the vitality of Christ's grace, and share enthusiasm for his message, you know that there is something even higher and more noble: hence it becomes possible for you to pray "not so much to be understood, as to understand; to be loved as to love." And so you are called to be leaders of the next generation through understanding and love. (175, p. 2)

Given a mandate of salvation. Every person receives from God a personal vocation, a particular mandate of salvation. Whatever form God's will for us assumes, it is, when all is said and done, always a joyful message for us, a message for our eternal salvation. This also holds true for you who are called as badly handicapped persons to a quite particular way of following him, the way of the cross. With the above-mentioned words Christ calls upon you to take your sorrows as his yoke, as a way of following in his footsteps. Only in this way will you not collapse under the weight of painful burdens. The only proper answer to God's call to follow Christ, whatever concrete form it may assume, is the answer of the Blessed Virgin: "Let it be done to me according to your word" (Lk 1:38). Only your prompt "yes" to God's will, which is often beyond our human comprehension, can make you blessed and bestow on you, even now, a deep joy that cannot be destroyed from outside by any necessity. (191, p. 5)

Each one of us is like a special kind of raw material from which—through following Christ—it is possible to fashion in the concrete this unique and absolutely singular form of life that can be called the Christian vocation. Much was said in the last Council on this point concerning the vocation of the laity. (160, p. 77)

In presenting the complete picture of the People of God and recalling the place among that people held not only by priests but also by the laity, not only by the representatives of the hierarchy but also by those of the institutes of consecrated life, the Second Vatican Council did not deduce this picture merely from a sociological premise. . . . For the whole of the community of the people of God and for each member of it what is in question is not just a specific "social membership"; rather, for each and every one what is essential is a particular "vocation." . . . It is the community of the disciples, each of whom in a different way— at times very consciously and consistently, at other times not very consciously and very inconsistently—is following Christ. (73, p. 641)

In the ordinary circumstances of life. Christ calls us to become fathers and mothers of a family, sons and daughters, doctors, engineers, lawyers, technicians, scientists, educators, students, pupils, anyone whomsoever! Each one has a place in this building up of the Body of Christ, just as each one has a place and a task in the building up of the common good of people, of society, of the nation, of humanity. The Church is building herself up in the world. She is building herself up with living people. At the beginning of my episcopal service, I ask each of you to find and define your own place in this work of construction. (14, p. 7)

Everyone's vocation is a mystery of God. My first message is for you, beloved young people, for you who keep the special call of Christ in your hearts as a powerful impulse. Always be aware of the predilection that this initiative of the divine Master signifies for you: every vocation is part of a great divine plan, in which each of those called is very important. Christ himself, the Word of God, the "Called" par excellence, "did not exalt himself to be made a high priest, but was appointed by him who said to him, 'Thou art my Son, today I have begotten Thee' [Ps 2:7]; as he says also in another place, 'Thou art a priest for ever, after the order of Melchizedek' [Ps 110:4]" (Heb 5:5).

Vocation is, therefore, a mystery that all accept and live in the depths of their being. A gift and a grace, it depends on supreme, divine freedom, and in its true reality, it escapes our understanding. We cannot demand explanations from the Giver of all goods—"Why have you made me thus?" (Rom 9:20)—because he who calls is also "He who is" (cf. Ex 3:14).

The vocation of each one merges, up to a certain point, with his or her very being: it can be said that vocation and person become just one thing. This means that in God's creative initiative there enters a particular act of love for those called not only to salvation but also to the ministry of salvation. Therefore, from all eternity, since we began to exist in the plans of the Creator and he willed us to be creatures, he also willed us to be "called," preparing in us the gifts and conditions for the personal, conscious, and opportune response to the call of Christ and of the Church. God who loves us, who is love, is also "He who calls" (cf. Rom 9:11).

Therefore, in the presence of a vocation, we adore the mystery, we respond lovingly to the initiative of love, we say "yes" to the call. (168, p. 6)

Each of us in society, but in particular in the Church, has a vocation and a responsibility of our own. Every Christian in the community of the People of God must contribute to the construction of the Body of Christ, which is the Church. This is the "kingly service" of which the Second Vatican Council speaks (cf. Dogmatic Constitution *Lumen Gentium,* no. 36), in accordance with which not only the Pope, Bishops, and Priests, but all Christians, that is, married couples, parents, men and women of different conditions and professions, must construct their lives. (93, p. 4)

Calling each one to decide for Christ. Yours is the age of responsible and deliberate meeting with Christ. Beloved youths, Jesus Christ alone is the adequate and ultimate answer to the supreme question about the meaning of life and history.

While respecting those who have other ideas, and well aware that faith in Christ has its times and its seasons and demands a personal development, bound up with God's grace, I tell you with confident frankness that having passed the ingenuous age of childhood and the sentimental period of adolescence and having arrived at youth, that is, your exuberant and critical age, the most beautiful and stirring adventure that can happen to you is the personal meeting with Jesus, who is the only one who gives real meaning to our life.

It is not enough to look; it is necessary to look in order to find certainty. And certainty is Jesus, who states: "I am the way, and the truth, and the life!" (Jn 14:6); "I am the light of the world; the one who follows me will not walk in darkness . . ." (Jn 8:12); "For this I have come into the world, to bear witness to the truth!" (Jn 18:37).

Only Jesus has convincing and consoling words; only he has words of life, in fact, of eternal life: "For God so loved the world that he gave his only Son, that whoever believes in him should not perish but have eternal life. For God sent the Son into the world, not to condemn the world, but that the world might be saved through him" (Jn 5:16–17).

Finally, and it is the practical conclusion, yours is the age of the most important decision. Whatever path you will choose in life, the most important decision is to live everywhere, always, and with everyone the Christian ideal of love for God and one's neighbor.

Do not move away from Christ! Decide to be for him! (76, p. 11)

I turn in a completely special way to the laity, namely, men, women, fathers, mothers, professionals, workers, young boys and girls, students. I recall the word that seventeen years ago Paul VI addressed to you alone, the faithful of Frascati, speaking of the maturity of conscience of the Catholic laity as regards the apostolate. This conscience, he stated, "is not given . . . only from the necessity of lengthening the arms of the priest who cannot be present in all areas and cannot encompass all works. It is given by something deeper and more essential, by the fact, that is, that the laity also is Christian. From within your conscience rings a voice: If I am a Christian, I must not be a negative element, passive and neutral and perhaps an adversary of the wave of the spirit that Christianity puts in souls" (*Insegnamenti di Paolo VI,* vol. 1 [1965], p. 570). (179, p. 3)

And leading to personal fulfillment. I want you all to be the best, the greatest persons you can be. I want you to develop to the full the immense possibilities that God has given you, when he made you in his own image. Do not be afraid. Do not be satisfied with mediocrity. (235, p. 6)

And you, dear young people, do you really feel, deeply, that you are the hope and the joyful promise of tomorrow? Certainly, awareness of youthfulness is not sufficient to give the sense of that inner confidence that alone makes it possible to look to the future with the calm certainty of being able to change the forces operating in the world, for the construction of a society really worthy of humanity.

To be young means living within oneself an incessant newness of spirit, nourishing a continual quest for good, releasing an impulse to change always for the better, realizing a persevering determination of dedication. Who will make all this possible for us? Do people have within themselves the strength to face with their own forces the snares of evil, selfishness, and—let us say so clearly—the disintegrating snares of the "prince of this world," who is always active to give human beings, first, a false sense of their autonomy, and then to bring them, through failure, to the abyss of despair?

All of us, the young and adults, must have recourse to Christ the eternally young, Christ the conqueror of every expression of death, Christ who rose again for ever, Christ who communicates in the Holy Spirit the continuous, irrepressible life of the Father; we must do so in order to found and ensure the hope of tomorrow, which you will build, but which is already potentially present today. (15, p. 1)

I sincerely hope that in our times, St. Catherine, Doctor of the Church, will continue to be the patroness of the awareness of the Christian vocation of everyone; an awareness that, in a particular way, must mature and be increased so that the Church can fulfill the mission entrusted to her by Christ, in accordance with the needs of our times.

In Saint Catherine of Siena, I see a visible sign of the mission of women in the Church. . . . The Church of Jesus Christ and of the apostles is at the same time a Church that is Mother and Spouse. These Biblical expressions clearly reveal how deeply the mission of women is inscribed in the mystery of the Church. And may we discover together the many-sided significance of this mission, going hand in hand with the world of women today and basing ourselves on the riches that from the beginning, the Creator placed in the heart of women, and on the wonderful wisdom of this heart, which God wished to reveal many centuries ago in Saint Catherine of Siena. (10, pp. 6–7)

Each One Has a Place in This Building Up of the Body of Christ

John Paul II reminds everyone of their personal and unique call: The handicapped. Above all, however, the Pope would like to express to you yourselves, dear disabled brothers and sisters, his deep sympathy and love, his high esteem, and the great confidence he places in you, in your help through prayer and sacrifice—particularly through the patient and self-sacrificing acceptance of your suffering.

Consider your fate in life above all with the eyes of faith. What seems to the unbeliever a tragic misfortune can become for the believer an extremely meaningful and fulfilling role in the midst of the human community and the Church. Our fate is not the result of blind chance, but has been intended or permitted by the loving God, and his quite personal call reaches us in it. (238, p. 12)

Artisans. I now address a cordial greeting to members of the pilgrimage of the Association of Artisans of the Province of Bergamo. I know very well, beloved children, that you wish to do honor to the Christian name, of which your land is proud. I exhort you, therefore, to love the Lord generously, to follow the life of the Church with attention and deep respect, putting into practice with sincere loyalty her teachings and directives, especially in the environments of your toils and your industry. Persevere with renewed fervor in this Christian witness. The Pope is close to you with his prayer and his affection, and blesses you willingly, together with all your dear ones. (184, p. 7)

Athletes. "Cycling implies and requires effort, a harmonious effort of the whole body, an effort the energy of which is shown less with the violence of leaps or blows than with the courage of human discipline and of steadfastness prolonged and sustained until the finishing line" (Pius XII, Address to participants of the twenty-ninth Cycle Tour of Italy, 2 June 1946).

I thank you, therefore, for your effort in this discipline, exhorting you to be concerned always with the complete development of your person. In particular, see to it that your competitions and your sporting ideal are always a help for your interior life, for the accomplishment of your social, family, and religious duties, especially, with the sanctification of the Sunday, by means of the meeting with Christ and in the commitment of communal charity. May you always be guided by a sincere commitment of true Christian life, of which modern society feels such need today. (162, p. 14)

Researchers. I stress here some fundamental points. Research at the university level presupposes all the loyalty, the seriousness, and for that very reason, the freedom of scientific investigation. It is at this price that you bear witness to the truth, that you serve the Church and society, that you deserve the esteem of the university world; and this in all branches of knowledge.

But when it is a question of the human being, of the field of human sciences, it is necessary to add the following: if it is right to take advantage of the contribution of the different methodologies, it is not sufficient to choose one, or even make a synthesis of several, to determine what the person is in depth. Christians cannot let themselves be hemmed in by them, all the more so in that they are not taken in by their premises. They know that they must go beyond the purely natural perspective; their faith makes them approach anthropology in the perspective of the person's full vocation and salvation; it is the light beneath which they work, the line that guides their research. In other words, a Catholic university is not only a field of religious research open in all directions; it presupposes in its teachers an anthropology enlightened by faith, consistent with faith, in particular with the Creation and with the Redemption of Christ. (69, p. 6)

Newlyweds. And finally, I thank the newlyweds for their presence, which is always so cordial and pleasing. You are always welcome, and you receive my best wishes for your new life together.

Also for you I wish to recall a thought of John Paul I, taken from one of his famous imaginary letters, published when he was still a cardinal: "The effort to see things from the better side should be the mark of the Christian; if it is true that "gospel" means good news, the Christian should be a happy person and one who radiates happiness" ("Illustrissimi," Letter to Hippocrates [Padova: ed. Messaggero, 1978], 198).

In your new life, my dear newlyweds, always try to see things from the better side, seek to understand each other, to confide to each other your joys and sorrows, to pray together, and so you will be happy and will be witnesses of the "good news." (114, p. 8)

Elderly. The Catholic Church willingly lends her support to efforts that encourage the elderly themselves to look with realism and serenity on the role that God has assigned to them. With the wisdom and experience of their lives they have entered a period of extraordinary grace, with new opportunities for prayer and union with God, having been endowed with new spiritual forces with which to serve others and to make a fervent offering of their lives to the Lord and Giver of life. Efforts, moreover, that are aimed at fostering and sponsoring programs on behalf of the elderly are worthy of the highest praise. Christ's teaching is clear; what is done for his brethren is done for him (cf. Mt 25:40), and its value is seen in this light. . . .

To proclaim the mission of the elderly and thereby to promote their special role in the human family is a task of great importance. The elderly are meant to be part of the social scene; their very existence gives an insight into God's creation and the functioning of society. The life of the aging helps to clarify a scale of human values; it shows the continuity of generations and marvelously demonstrates the interdependence of God's people. The elderly often have the charism to bridge generation gaps before they are made; how many children have found understanding and love in the eyes and words and caresses of the aging? And how many old people have willingly subscribed to the inspired word that "the crown of the aged is their children's children" (Prv 17:6). (178, p. 3)

Prisoners. In you I find human beings, and I know that every human being corresponds to a "thought" of God. In this sense, every human being is fundamentally good and made for happiness. There was in the life of nearly all of you a moment in which you departed from God's plan. You should regret the wrong done, but not consider it an evil destiny. You can return to reflecting God's thought. You can be happy again.

I find in you people redeemed by the precious blood of Jesus Christ. This blood speaks to you of the infinite love of the Father and of his Son Jesus for you as for all. He offers you the greatest joy in the world, which is that of loving and of feeling oneself loved. From above, he gives you the strength necessary to change your life.

I find in you real brothers and sisters, and I want to tell you that in moments of loneliness and sadness, you can be certain you can have the certainty that this common Father is close to you and that in him you can find all your brothers and sisters, who are the Christians and Catholics of the whole world. (163, p. 7)

Teachers. The Catholic university must be an environment in which Christianity is alive and operating. It is an essential vocation of the Catholic university to bear witness that it is a community seriously . . . engaged in scientific research, but also visibly characterized by a real Christian life. . . . That presupposes, among other things, a revision of the figure of the professor, who cannot be considered a mere transmitter of knowledge, but also and above all a witness and educator to true Christian life. In this privileged environment of formation, you, dear students, are called to conscientious and responsible collaboration, free and generous, to realize your formation itself. (59, p. 5)

Youth. I would like to recommend one thing to you: live these years of yours with commitment and with joy, so that they will not be empty, but rich in content; live them in study, in prayer, and in the deepening of your Christian faith, and also in physical exercise to maintain good health. Only in this way can they constitute a valuable and fruitful reserve for future years. (228, p. 3)

Domestic workers. Each of you represents hidden work that is necessary and indispensable, work of sacrifice, not exciting, which does not win applause and sometimes does not even have recognition and gratitude: the humble, repeated, monotonous, and therefore heroic work of an innumerable host who with their daily labor contribute to the budget of so many families and solve so many difficult and delicate situations, helping distant parents or brothers or sisters in need.

And the pope who has known the hardships of life is with you, understands you, esteems you, accompanies you in your aspirations and desires, and hopes with all his heart. . . .

This gives rise also to the dignity of your work as family collaborators: your commitment is not a humiliation but a consecration! In fact, you collaborate directly in the smooth running of the family; and this is a great task, one would say almost a mission. For this, adequate preparation and maturity are necessary in order to be competent in the various household activities; to rationalize work and get to know family psychology; to learn the so-called "pedagogy of fatigue," which makes it possible to organize one's services better; and also to exercise the necessary educating function. It is a whole world, extremely important and precious, that opens up to your eyes and to your responsibilities every day. I praise, therefore, all those engaged in domestic activity and you family collaborators, who give your ability and your labor for the good of the home.

There is no law that lays it down that you must smile! But you can make a gift of your smile; you can be the leaven of kindness in the family. Remember what St. Paul wrote to the first Christians: "Whatever you do, in word or deed, do everything in the name of the Lord Jesus, giving thanks to God the Father through him" (Col 3:17). "Whatever your task, work heartily, as serving the Lord and not others, knowing that from the Lord you will receive the inheritance as your reward" (Col 3:23–24). Love your work. Love the persons with whom you collaborate! From love and goodness there will spring also your joy and satisfaction. (98, pp. 31–32)

The sick. Beloved! My pastoral visit, so near to Holy Week, thus becomes a meditation on the "Passion of Christ" and on the "Passion of human beings." Reflecting on the Divine Word, who goes through the anguish of Gethsemane and the agony of the cross to redeem us from the darkness of error and evil, we understand why all of us too must go through the Calvary of suffering. Until the second coming of Christ, the redemption is being accomplished, day by day. I welcome the opportunity to express my hearty congratulations for all the modern resources adopted to meet the needs of the sick, to develop their possibilities, to make them self-sufficient as much as can be hoped, caring for them and making them responsible; and at the same time I encourage and exhort you to make use of every physio- and psychotherapeutic technology with care and good will. Yet I am urged also to remind you that despite all the conquests of science, the "Passion of Christ," together with the "Passion of human beings," endures in history in the role and in the prospective of the final resurrection in Christ for all who have believed in him and have loved and suffered with him. . . .

You too, the sick, relatives and friends, transform your "passion" into an act of redemptive love; offer it every day and raise it to the Most High as the priest at the altar offers the pure and spotless host and the cup of eternal salvation! (265, p. 7)

CHAPTER 2

THE CONDITION OF THE LAITY

What fear weighs on the people of our time!

The world is full of fear, and efforts to improve our world are frequently lacking. Many have an inadequate view of person. Others are chained in slavery. Vast numbers become anonymous, faceless, and exploited, and we witness the primacy of technology over culture; this is a painful sign of our times, and more than ever we need to experience love and understanding.

Development projects must always have a human face.

We must reemphasize the primacy of person and urge all peoples to cooperate in this. The Church knows her responsibility, is close to struggling humanity, appeals on their behalf, and offers all spiritual support and direction.

Create around you wide spaces of humanity.

Evangelization leads to freedom, reveals the true meaning of life, and integrates faith and culture. Faithful Christians are also good citizens, whatever their life situation and profession—work, study, sport, community service, farming—but they are also there as a presence of Christ.

Reach peace, teach peace!

Peace has become a major preoccupation, but we must reach peace through concrete and specific efforts. We must offer to the world visions of peace.

What Fear Weighs on the People of Our Time!

The world is full of fear. Yet what fear weighs on the people of our time! It is a multiple concern, characterized precisely by fear of the future, of a possible self-destruction of humanity, and then, also, more generally, fear of a certain type of materialistic civilization, which puts things before persons, and again, by the fear of being victims of abuses and oppressions that deprive the person of internal and external freedom. Well, only Christ frees us from all this and enables us to raise our spirits, to find hope again, to have confidence in ourselves to the extent to which we have confidence in him: "Look to him, and be radiant" (Ps 34 [33]:5). (210, p. 3)

But we recoil from death. We are afraid of death. We defend ourselves from death. And society tries to defend us from death.

Progress, which has been constructed by generations of people with so much difficulty, with the waste of so much energy and at such a cost, contains, however, in its complexity, a powerful factor of death. It even conceals within it a gigantic potential for death. Is it necessary to prove this in a society that is aware of what possibilities of destruction there are in modern military and nuclear arsenals?

The modern person, therefore, is afraid. The superpowers, who have those arsenals at their disposal, are afraid, and the others—continents, nations, cities . . . are afraid.

This fear is justified. Not only do there exist possibilities of destruction and slaughter unknown before, but today already human beings are killing each other in large numbers! They are killing in homes, in offices, in universities. Armed with modern weapons they are killing defenseless and innocent people. Incidents of this kind have always occurred, but today this has become a system. If people affirm that it is necessary to kill others in order to change and improve humanity and society, then we must ask whether, together with this gigantic material progress in which our age participates, we have not arrived simultaneously at the point of wiping out humanity itself, a value so fundamental and elementary! Have we not already arrived at the denial of that fundamental and elementary principle, which the ancient Christian thinker [Irenaeus] expressed in the sentence "Humanity must live"? (145, p. 3)

And efforts to improve our world are frequently lacking. I am afraid that many good desires to construct a just society founder on the lack of authenticity and burst like a bubble when they are not sustained by a serious commitment of austerity and frugality. In other words, it is necessary to overcome the temptation of the so-called "consumer society," the temptation of the ambition to have more and more, instead of trying to be more and more; the ambition to have more and more while others have less and less. In this connection, I think that the beatitude of the poor in spirit should take on concrete meaning and power in your lives: in the rich young people so that they will understand that the superfluous things they have are nearly always what others lack, and that they may not go away sorrowfully (cf. Mt 19:22) if they hear in the depths of their consciences a call of the Lord to fuller detachment; in the young persons who are living the hard experience of uncertainty of the future, who may even suffer the pangs of hunger, so that seeking to improve, as their right, the living standards of their families and of themselves, they may be attracted by human dignity, not by ambition, greed, and the fascination of the superfluous.

My friends, you are also responsible for the preservation of the real values that have always done honor to the Brazilian people. Do not let yourselves be swept away by the provocation of sex, which compromises the authenticity of human love and leads to the disintegration of the family. "Do you not know that you are God's temple and that God's Spirit dwells in you?" St. Paul wrote in the text we have heard read to us.

Let girls try to find true feminism, the real fulfillment of woman as a human being, as an integral part of the family and as a member of society, in conscious participation, according to her characteristics. (164, p. 2)

Many have an inadequate view of the person. Perhaps one of the most obvious weaknesses of present-day civilization lies in an inadequate view of the person. Without doubt, our age is the one in which humanity has been most written and spoken of, the age of the forms of humanism and the age of anthropocentrism. Nevertheless, it is, paradoxically, also the age of humanity's deepest anxiety about its identity and its destiny, the age of humanity's abasement to previously unsuspected levels, the age of human values trampled on as never before. (51, p. 534)

City life today makes human relationships difficult, because everyone is out of breath from a never-ending race between the place where they work, the family lodging, and the places where they go shopping. The integration of children, young, and old people often gives rise to acute problems. These are appeals to work together to create ever more human living conditions for all. (158, p. 55)

Others are chained in slavery. How could I forget the innumerable victims of drugs, which are offered from the first years of adolescence and then become an iron chain of shameful slavery? How to forget the moral devastations that an equally ignoble industry or a permissive and hedonistic mentality, which permeates part of the publishing world and the communications media through the image, have produced in the spirit of so many young people who take unbridled hedonism as their norm of life? How to forget the manipulation of the human personality in formation through the mass media, ideological indoctrination, the partial and distorted presentation of the truth, pornography?

On all these alarming symptoms of moral regression there is grafted the factor of violence, in all its stages, which obeys solely a logic of destruction and death and which might, God forbid, paralyze the common aspiration to orderly progress, constructive concord, industrious peace. To these young people, who today are not afraid to kill or wound other young people, other human beings, I address on my knees, like my predecessor Paul VI, the cry of hope and the invitation that I let ring out at Drogheda: "I appeal to young people who may have become caught up in organizations engaged in violence. I say to you, with all the love I have for you, with all the trust I have in young people: Do not listen to voices that speak the language of hatred, revenge, retaliation. . . . The true courage lies in working for peace. The true strength lies in joining with the young men and women of your generation everywhere in building up a just and human and Christian society by the ways of peace. Violence is the enemy of justice. Only peace can lead to true justice." (138, pp. 503–504)

Vast numbers become anonymous, faceless, and exploited. Today, the problem of work has taken on world proportions: "While in the past," as I wrote at the beginning of the encyclical [*Laborem Exercens*, no. 2], "the *class* question was specially highlighted at the center of this issue, in more recent times it is the *world* question that is emphasized. Thus not only the sphere of class is taken into consideration, but also the world dimension of the tasks involved in the path toward the achievements of justice in the modern world."

In this perspective, which cannot be compared with any other period of history, you understand very well, Your Excellencies, ladies and gentlemen, that the great danger that weighs upon the evolution of social life today is constituted above all by the fact that such enormous and complex mechanisms, now of international dimensions, threaten humanity actually and seriously. Human beings who must be at the center of common interest, those who, according to God's original plan, are called to become the masters of the earth, to "subdue" it (Gn 1:28) through the superiority of their intelligence and the strength of their physical labor, run the risk of being reduced to the state of instruments, of becoming anonymous and faceless pieces of machinery, until they are crushed by forces greater than themselves, which can be used to their detriment to dominate the masses pressed down by need, by others who play with interests contrary to the good of the person and manipulate the latter at their pleasure.

That is why I wished to recall in the first place that each one remains the subject of work precisely as a person. I emphasized the fact that when a one-sided, materialistic civilization prevails, in which the subjective dimension of work is relegated to a secondary plan, the person is treated as an instrument of production. Now, in actual fact, independent of the work carried out, the person should be considered its efficient subject and its real creator and artisan. In this light, stress must be laid on the trade union rights of the world of work in view of the defense of a just wage and of the security of the person of the worker and of the worker's family. They are rights that are opposed to the totalitarian tendencies of every system or organization that aims at suffocating them or diverting them to its own advantage.

The real responsibility for the humanization of working conditions in every country is incumbent in the first place on the public authorities. And there is formed, furthermore, a network of exchanges and dependencies that influence international life and are capable of creating various forms of legalized exploitation, so to speak. It is well known, in fact, that highly industrialized countries establish prices as high as possible for their products, seeking at the same time to keep the prices of raw materials and semi-manufactured products as low as possible. It is for this reason, among others, that there is an ever-increasing disproportion between the national income of rich countries and those of the poorest countries. (257, p. 563)

Dear friends: in fidelity to these principles the Church wants to call attention to a very grave, current situation—the problem of emigrants. We cannot ignore the condition of millions of people who, in search of work and their own bread, must leave their homeland, often their families, to face the hardships of new surroundings that are not always pleasant or welcoming, to face an unfamiliar language and general conditions that bring loneliness and discrimination to them, their spouses, and their families.

It happens that some people take advantage of them by offering lower wages, cutting social security benefits and other social aid, and by providing housing unsuited to human dignity. Again, it is often felt that first the greatest yield must be wrested from the migrant worker without regard for the human being within.

The church continues to teach that the approach to take in this and similar fields is that economic, social, and political interests not be placed above each person. Rather, the dignity of the human being must prevail above all other things, which in turn must be subservient to the person (60, p. 558)

And we witness the primacy of technology over culture; this is a painful sign of our times. When innocent people die, when society lives in a state of threat, then it reveals its worst face; not the struggle for the good of humanity, but the struggle against humanity.

Is not this struggle—from various standpoints—"a painful sign of our times"?

Therefore, that "sign of contradiction," born of the prayer of Christ himself and dictated by love for humanity, is indispensable.

"Do not be overcome by evil, but overcome evil with good," the Apostle says (Rom 12:21).

In an age in which the different programs of the struggle for humanity often assume threatening forms of struggle against humanity, it is necessary to strive for the rapprochement of people, for their union on the basis of respect of what is essentially and deeply human. (42, p. 2)

Science and technology have always formed part of humanity's culture, but today we are witnessing the speedily increasing growth of a technology that seems to have destroyed its equilibrium with the dimensions of culture by acting as an element of division. Such is the great problem facing modern society. Science and technology are the most dynamic factors of the development of society today, but their intrinsic limitations do not make them capable, by themselves, of providing a power that will bind culture together. How then can a culture absorb science and technology, with their dynamism, without losing its own identity?

There are three temptations to be avoided in this regard. The first is the temptation to pursue technological development for its own sake, the sort of development that has for its only norm that of its own growth and affirmation, as if it were a matter of an independent reality in between nature and a reality that is properly human, imposing on people the inevitable realization of their ever-new possibilities, as if one should always do what is technically possible. The second temptation is that of subjecting technological development to economic usefulness in accordance with the logic of profit or nonstop economic expansion, thus creating advantages for some while leaving others in poverty, with no care for the true common good of humanity, making technology into an instrument at the service of the ideology of "having." Thirdly, there is also the temptation to subject technological development to the pursuit or maintenance of power, as happens when it is used for military purposes and whenever people are manipulated in order that they may be dominated. (221, p. 16)

As scholars and researchers, you represent an international community, with a task that can be decisive for the future of humanity. But on one condition: that you succeed in defending and serving humanity's true culture as a precious possession. Your role is a noble one, when you work toward the growth of individuals in their being and not just in their possessions or their knowledge or their power. It is in the depths of the person's being that true human culture lies. I tried to express this fundamental aspect of our civilization in an address that I gave to UNESCO on 2 June 1980: "Culture is a specific way of human *existing* and *being*. . . . Culture is that through which the person is more, has more access to being. The fundamental distinction between what the person is and what the person has, between being and having, has its foundation there too. . . . All human *having* is important for culture, is a factor creative of culture, only to the extent to which the person, through having, can at the same time *be* more fully as a person, become more fully a person in all the dimensions of his existence, in everything that characterizes his or her humanity." This concept of culture is based upon a total view of the human being, body and spirit, person and community, a rational being and one ennobled by love: "Yes! the future of humanity depends on culture! Yes! the peace of the world depends on the primacy of the Spirit! Yes! the peaceful future of humankind depends on love!" In truth, our future, our very survival, are linked to the image that we shall make of humanity. (221, p. 16)

And more than ever we need to experience love and understanding. The modern world, in fact, is in great need of friendship, understanding, love, and charity. So bring your charity, your love, your help, with perseverance and sensitivity! It is charity that saves and becomes the way to truth! It is being realized more and more that the young person caught up in the poisonous spirals of drugs has an essential need to feel loved and understood in order to be rehabilitated and to resume the normal way of those who accept life in the perspective of eternity. But above all, be vehicles of, and witnesses to, the love and mercy of God, the friend who does not betray and who continues to love and to wait with confident hope. How true and moving are the words written by St. Thérèse of the Child Jesus in her last illness: "Yes, I feel it; if I had on my conscience all the sins that can be committed, I would throw myself all the same into the arms of Jesus, my heart overcome with repentance, because I know how much he loves the prodigal child who returns to him" (Ms. C).

Beloved in Christ! Here is your task and your orders; bring confidence and love! (174, p. 4)

Development Projects Must Always Have a Human Face

We must reemphasize the primacy of person. It is no use complaining of the wickedness of the times. As St. Paul wrote, we must overcome evil by doing good (Rom 12:21). The world esteems and respects the courage of ideas and the strength of virtues. Do not be afraid to refuse words, acts, and attitudes that are not in conformity with Christian ideals. Be courageous in rejecting what destroys your innocence or wilts the freshness of your love for Christ.

To seek, love, and bear witness to Jesus! This is your commitment; these are the instructions I leave you! By doing so, not only will you keep real joy in your lives, but also you will benefit the whole of society, which needs, above all, consistency with the evangelical message. (11, p. 1)

It becomes necessary, therefore, on the part of all to recover an awareness of the primacy of moral values, which are the values of the human being as such. The great task that has to be faced today for the renewal of society is that of recapturing the ultimate meaning of life and its fundamental values. Only an awareness of the primacy of these values enables human beings to use the immense possibilities given them by science in such a way as to bring about the true advancement of the human being in his or her whole truth, in his or her freedom and dignity. Science is called to ally itself with wisdom. (250, p. 441)

Development projects must always have a human face. They cannot be reduced to a purely materialistic or economic endeavor. The human being must always be the ultimate measure of the feasibility and the success of an economic or social program. Progress can therefore not be separated from the dignity of the human being or from the respect for his or her fundamental rights. In the pursuit of progress, total progress, anything must be rejected that is unworthy of the freedom and the human rights of the individual and of the people as a whole. Thus are rejected such elements as corruption, bribery, embezzlement of public funds, domination over the weak, callousness toward the poor and handicapped. Participation in the political life of the country; freedom of religion, of speech, of association; the protection of a well-functioning judiciary system; respect for and promotion of things spiritual and cultural; love of truth. These are the ingredients for progress that is truly and fully human. (258, p. 591)

The construction of a new social order presupposes, over and above the essential technological skills, a lofty inspiration, a courageous motivation, belief in humanity's future, in its dignity, in its destiny. It is the human heart and spirit that must be reached, beyond the divisions spawned by individual interests, selfishness, and ideologies. In a word, human beings must be loved for their own sake. This is the supreme value that all sincere humanists, generous thinkers, and all the great religions want to promote. Love for the person as such is at the center of the message of Jesus Christ and his Church: this relationship is indissoluble. In my speech to UNESCO, I stressed the fundamental link between the gospel and human beings in their very humanity: "This link is in fact a creator of culture in its very foundation. . . . Persons must be affirmed for themselves. . . . What is more, persons must be loved because they are human; love must be claimed for human beings by reason of the particular dignity they possess. The whole of the affirmations concerning human beings belongs to the very substance of Christ's message and of the mission of the Church" (Address to UNESCO, June 2, 1980, no. 10).

All those who desire the defence and progress of humanity must therefore love human beings for their own sake; and for this it is essential to count upon the values of the spirit, which are alone capable of transforming hearts and deeply-rooted attitudes. All of us who bear in our hearts the treasure of a religious faith must share in the common work of humanity's development, and we must do it with clear-sightedness and courage. All Christians, all those who call upon God, all spiritual families, should be invited to join in a common effort to sustain, spiritually and culturally, all those men and women who devote themselves to the total growth of humanity. (221, pp. 16–17)

And urge all peoples to cooperate in this. This full spiritual dimension is too often neglected or absent nowadays in the enterprises of people and nations. It is absent in its deep totality. It is absent when a society withdraws into itself and aims at goals from which only a part of the people benefit, to the detriment of others. Becoming deeply and often painfully aware of this, many people of goodwill, many Christians, . . . do not hesitate to dedicate their attention and their strength to the great task of the real development of humanity and peoples, which appears as an immense challenge. For every day brings new obstacles on the way to integral human development, and you can make a list of them. Certainly, there are plenty of theories and approaches that encourage humanity's progress, but often in a partial way; or they try to satisfy material needs to the detriment of cultural and spiritual values. It is in this context that we can discover the specific vocation that is ours. We must, in the first place, look at the real problems and the technical, scientific, or political means proposed to bring solutions, full in the face. But our specific role as Christians, the role of the Church, is to compare these possibilities with the principles of humanity, of humanity's real nature and destiny, and of its transcendent vocation. (189, p. 8)

I would like to exhort each of you and, through you, all the leaders of the nations that you represent, to eliminate fear and mistrust and replace them with mutual trust, welcome vigilance, and communal collaboration. This new atmosphere in relations among the nations will make it possible to discover areas of agreement that are often unsuspected.

Allow the Pope, this humble pilgrim of peace that I am, to call your attention again to the appeal I made, in my message for the Day of Peace, to all those responsible for the fate of nations. Do not hesitate to commit yourselves personally for peace with acts of peace, each in your own sphere and in your own sphere of responsibility. Create new and bold acts that are manifestations of respect, community, confidence, and welcome. By means of these acts you will use all your personal and professional capacities in the service of the great cause of peace. And I promise you that along the way to peace, you will always find God accompanying you. (49, p. 3)

On the other hand, the Church and the Holy See, in particular, ask your nations, your governments, to take increasingly into consideration a certain number of needs. The Holy See does not seek this for itself. It does so in union with the local episcopate, for the Christians or believers who inhabit your countries, in order that without any special privilege but in all justice they may nourish their faith, ensure religious worship, and be admitted as loyal citizens to full participation in social life. The Holy See does so also in the interest of all people, whoever they may be, knowing that freedom; respect for life and dignity of persons, who are never instruments; fairness in treatment; professional conscientiousness in work; and a united pursuit of the common good, the spirit of reconciliation, opening to spiritual values, are fundamental requirements of harmonious life in society and of the progress of citizens and their civilization. Certainly the last-mentioned goals generally figure on the program of those responsible. But the result, for all that, cannot be taken for granted, and all means are not equally valid. There are still too many physical and moral miseries that depend on negligence, selfishness, and the blindness or hardness of people. The Church wishes to contribute to diminish these miseries with her peaceful means, by education to the moral sense, by the loyal action of Christians and persons of good will. Doing so, the Church may sometimes not be understood, but she is convinced that she is rendering a service that humanity cannot do without. She is faithful to her Teacher and Savior, Jesus Christ. (2, p. 3)

The initiative undertaken by you in your reflections and discussions during these days will necessarily also involve giving its whole value to an ethical imperative that challenges both individuals in their personal behavior and witness, and citizens and politicians in their public acts aimed at setting up structures that are human in dimension. It is an ethical imperative that aims at preventing anyone from shirking his or her responsibility, with a view to ensuring the primacy of the human. It is precisely from a continually renewed moral consciousness that there arises a new hope, the "Nova Spes." And it alone will be capable of mobilizing all living forces, all people of goodwill, to exalt together what is most human in people and to work together for the purpose of asserting it in historical praxis and in the reality of relations between peoples. (185, p. 4)

The Church knows her responsibility. The Church's responsibility for divine truth must be increasingly shared in various ways by all. What shall we say at this point with regard to the specialists in the various levels and with different specializations? As members of the People of God, they all have their own part to play in Christ's prophetic mission and service of divine truth, among other ways by an honest attitude toward truth, whatever field it may belong to, while educating others in truth and teaching them to mature in love and justice. Thus, a sense of responsibility for truth is one of the fundamental points of encounter between the Church and each person and also one of the fundamental demands determining each one's vocation in the community of the Church. (73, p. 639)

Faith does not offer resources to scientific research as such, but it encourages scientists to pursue their research knowing that they meet, in nature, the presence of the Creator. (83, p. 8)

"The reason I was born, the reason why I came into the world, is to testify to the truth" (Jn 18:37). The Church, looking to Christ, who bears witness to the truth, must always and everywhere ask herself and, in a certain sense, the contemporary world too, how to make good emerge from humanity, how to liberate the dynamism of the good that is in humanity so that it will be stronger than evil, any moral, social evil, etc. We want not only to recommend this effort to God, but also to follow it for the good of the Church and of the whole human family. (68, pp. 600–602)

Humanity's hope and the hope of the modern world, the prospect of a really "better, more human future," depend on the "Confiteor" and the "Kyrie Eleison." They depend on conversion: on the many, many human conversions that are capable of transforming not only each one's personal life but the life of environments and of the whole of society, from the smallest to ever-larger environments, until it comprises the whole human family. (204, p. 4)

Is close to struggling humanity. As you well know, the commitment and the effort to interpret the thirst for justice and dignity that men and women feel deeply in modern times are also part of the vocation of the Church. And in this function of proclaiming and upholding the fundamental rights in all stages of human existence, the Church is comforted by the international community. (65, p. 6)

The Church shares with the people of our time this profound and ardent desire for a life that is just in every aspect, nor does she fail to examine the various aspects of the sort of justice that the life of people and society demands. This is confirmed by the field of Catholic social doctrine, greatly developed in the course of the last century. On the lines of this teaching proceed the education and formation of human consciences in the spirit of justice, and also individual undertakings, especially in the sphere of the apostolate of the laity, which are developing in precisely this spirit. (197, p. 412)

Wherever she is, the Church must sink her roots deeply into the spiritual and cultural soil of the country, assimilate all genuine values, enriching them also with the insights that she received from Jesus Christ, who is "the way and the truth and the life" (Jn 14:6) for all humanity. The Church's members will be at one and the same time good Christians and good citizens, making their contribution to the building up of the society of which they are full members. They will want to be, in every society, the best sons and daughters of their homeland, working unselfishly in collaboration with the others for the true good of the country. (220, p. 612)

Reflection that is inspired by science and by the wisdom of the world

scientific community must enlighten humanity regarding the consequences—good and bad—of scientific research and especially of that
research that concerns humanity, so that on the one hand there will be
no fixation on anticultural positions that retard the progress of humanity,
and that on the other hand there will be no attack on humanity's most
precious possession: the dignity of the person, destined to true progress
in the unity of the person's physical, intellectual, and spiritual well-being.
(239, p. 279)

And I wanted to come here just because it is a poor area, in order
that you might have the opportunity—I would say to which you have
the best claim—of being with the Pope. He sees in you a more living
presence of the Lord, who suffers in our neediest brothers, who continues to proclaim blessed the poor in spirit, those who suffer for justice
and are pure in heart, who work for peace, have compassion, and keep
their hope in Christ the Savior.

But on calling you to cultivate these spiritual and evangelical values,
I wish to make you think of your dignity as human beings and children
of God. I wish to encourage you to be rich in humanity, in love for the
family, in solidarity with others. At the same time, I exhort you to develop more and more the possibilities you have of obtaining a situation
of greater human and Christian dignity.

But what I have to say does not end here. The sight of the reality in
which you live must make so many people think of what can be done
effectively to remedy your condition.

On behalf of these brothers and sisters of ours, I ask all those who
can do so to help them to overcome their present situation, in order
that—particularly with a better education—they may improve their minds
and their hearts and be architects of their own elevation and of a more
advantageous integration in society. (48, p. 10)

Appeals on their behalf. The good of human beings—human beings
seen in the totality of their nature and in the full dignity of each person—is indeed a determining factor for all human interventions in this
field. Those who would serve humanity must be motivated by a love
and a compassion that effectively takes into account human beings in
their origin, in their composition, in the laws that govern their nature,
in the incomparable role that is theirs at the present time, as well as in
the grandeur of their destiny. It is this last factor that—far from negating
the value of the present moment or that of the future—seeks to put it
in full and final perspective. The sacredness of human life and its trans-

mission, the inviolability of all human rights, the importance of each individual person, all of this together is the perspective from which every intervention in the field of population and the urban future is rightfully evaluated; these are the criteria of its utility and its success.

Society today and tomorrow exists for all people and for the advancement of each one's personal dignity. (177, p. 6)

Particular care must be given to forming a social conscience at all levels and in all sectors. When injustices worsen and the distance between rich and poor increases distressingly, the social doctrine, in a form that is creative and open to the broad fields of the Church's presence, must be a valuable instrument for formation and action. This holds good particularly for the laity: "It is to the laity, though not exclusively to them, that secular duties and activity properly belong" (Constitution *Gaudium et Spes*, no. 43). It is necessary to avoid supplanting the laity and to study seriously just when certain forms of assistance to them retain their reason for existence. (51, p. 538)

Culture is an expression of humanity, a confirmation of humanity. Human beings create culture and through culture create themselves. They create themselves with the inward effort of the spirit, of thought, will, and heart. At the same time they create culture in communion with others. Culture is an expression of communication, of shared thought and collaboration, by human beings. It is born of service of the common good and becomes an essential good of human communities. (103, p. 58)

I think it can be considered a duty of justice and charity to make a resolute and persevering effort to husband energy resources and respect nature, not only so that humanity as a whole today may benefit, but also the generations to come. We are bound in solidarity to the generations to come. And I hope that Christians, moved particularly by gratitude to God, by the conviction that life and the world have a meaning, by unlimited hope and charity, will be the first to appreciate this duty and draw the necessary conclusions. (188, pp. 16–17)

And offers all spiritual support and direction. Life is a test. Giving human life this "paschal" meaning, that is, that it is a passing over, that it is a passing over to freedom. Jesus Christ taught with his word and even more with his own example that it is a test. The test corresponds to the importance of the forces accumulated in humanity. Humanity is created "for" the test, and called to it right from the beginning. It is necessary to think deeply of this call, meditating on the first chapters of the Bible, especially the first three. Human beings are described there not only as beings created "in the image of God" (Gen 1:26–27), but at the same time they are described as beings who undergo a test. And this is—if we analyze the text properly—the test of thought, of the heart and of the will, the test of truth and love. In this sense, it is at the same time the test of the Covenant with God. When this first Covenant was broken, God made another one. Today's readings recall the Covenant with Abraham, which was a way of preparation for the coming of Christ.

Christ confirms this meaning of life; it is humanity's great test. And for this very reason it has a meaning for humanity. It has not a meaning, on the contrary, if we believe that in life human beings must only take advantage, use, take, and even struggle implacably for the right to take advantage, use, take.

Life has its meaning when it is considered and lived as a test of an ethical character. Christ confirms this meaning and at the same time defines the adequate dimension of this test that human life is. Let us reread carefully, for example, the Sermon on the Mount, and also chapter 25 of Matthew's Gospel, the image of the judgment. This alone is enough to renew in us the fundamental Christian consciousness of the meaning of life.

The concept of "test" is closely connected with the concept of responsibility. Both are addressed to our will, to our acts. Accept, dear friends, both these concepts—or rather both realities—as elements of the construction of one's own humanity. (89, p. 8)

A great tension exists in the modern world. All things considered, this is a tension over the sense of human life, the meaning we can and must give to this life if it is to be worthy of human beings, if it is to be such that it is worth living. There also exist clear symptoms of moving away from these dimensions; in fact, materialism in different forms, inherited from the last centuries, is capable of coercing this meaning of life. But materialism does not at all form the deepest roots of European or world culture. It is not at all a correlative or a full expression of epistemological or ethical realism.

Christ—allow me to put it in this way—is the greatest realist in the history of humanity. Reflect a little on this formulation. Meditate on what it can signify.

It is precisely by virtue of this realism that Christ bears witness to the Father and bears witness to humanity. He himself, in fact, knows "what is in each person" (Jn 2:25). He knows! I repeat it without wishing to offend any of those who have tried at any time or are trying today to understand what the human being is and wish to teach it.

And precisely on the basis of this realism, Christ teaches that human life has a meaning insofar as it is a testimony of truth and love. (89, p. 8)

For this reason it is now fitting to reflect on this mystery. It is called for by the varied experiences of the Church and of contemporary humanity. It is also demanded by the pleas of many human hearts, their sufferings and hopes, their anxieties and expectations. While it is true that every individual human being is, as I said in the encyclical *Redemptor Hominis,* the way for the Church, at the same time the gospel and the whole of tradition constantly show us that we must travel this way with every individual, just as Jesus traced it out by revealing in himself the Father of his love. In Jesus Christ, every path to humanity, as it has been assigned once and for all to the Church in the changing context of the times, is simultaneously an approach to the Father and his love. The Second Vatican Council has confirmed this truth for our time. (197, p. 403)

Therefore, the times in which we live need you, Immaculate Mother of the Savior, who for all generations do not cease to be the sign of the advent of God and the sign of human hope.

Pope Pius XII, who in the horrible times of the Second World War dedicated the whole of mankind to your Immaculate Heart, found himself before this sign.

He who by divine will today is his successor in the Roman See puts himself before this sign and says:

"O Mother of individuals and peoples, you know all their sufferings and their hopes, you feel in a motherly way all the struggles between good and evil, between light and darkness, that shake the world—accept our cry addressed in the Holy Spirit directly to your heart and embrace with the love of the Mother and Handmaid of the Lord the people who are most awaiting this embrace, and at the same time the people whose trust you also particularly expect. Take under your motherly protection the whole human family, which we entrust to you with affectionate joy, O Mother. May the time of peace and freedom, the time of truth, justice, and hope approach for everyone." (249, p. 2)

The Church, an expert in humanity, faithful to the signs of the times, and in obedience to the pressing call of the last Council, wishes to continue today her mission of faith and defense of human rights. She calls upon Christians to commit themselves to the construction of a more just, human, and habitable world, which is not shut up within itself, but opens to God.

To construct this more just world means, among other things, making every effort in order that there will be no children without sufficient food, without education, without instruction; that there will be no young people without a suitable preparation; that, in order to live and to develop in a worthy way, there will be no peasants without land; that there will be no workers ill-treated or deprived of their rights; that there will be no systems that permit the exploitation of anyone by another person or by the State; that there will be no corruption; that there will be no persons living in superabundance while others through no fault of their own lack everything; that there will not be so many families badly formed, broken, disunited, receiving insufficient care; that there will be no injustice and inequality in the administration of justice; that there will be no one without the protection of the law, and that the law will protect all alike; that force will not prevail over truth and law, but truth and law over force; and that economic and political matters will never prevail over human matters.

But do not be content with this more human world. Make a world that is explicitly more divine, more in accordance with God, ruled by faith, and in which this latter inspires the moral, religious, and social progress of humanity. (46, p. 9)

Create Around You Wide Spaces of Humanity

Evangelization leads to freedom. To evangelize means making Christ present in the life of each one as a person, and at the same time in the life of society. To evangelize means doing everything possible, according to our capacities, in order that all "may believe;" in order that human beings may find themselves again in Christ; in order that they may find again in themselves the meaning and the adequate dimension of their own lives. This finding again is, at the same time, the deepest source of humanity's liberation. St. Paul expresses this when he writes: "For freedom, Christ has set us free" (Gal 5:1). So liberation, then, is certainly a reality of faith, one of the fundamental biblical themes, which are a deep part of Christ's salvific mission, of the work of Redemption, of his teaching. This subject has never ceased to constitute the content of the spiritual life of Christians. The Conference of the Latin American Episcopate bears witness that this subject returns in a new historical context; therefore, it must be taken up again in the teaching of the Church, in theology, and in the apostolate. It must be taken up again in its own depth, and in its evangelical authenticity. . . .

So this service of truth as participation in Christ's prophetic service is a task of the Church, which tries to carry it out in the various historical contexts. It is necessary to call by their name injustice, the exploitation of human beings by human beings, or the exploitation of human beings by the State, institutions, mechanisms of systems, and regimes, which sometimes operate without sensitivity. It is necessary to call by name every social injustice, discrimination, violence, inflicted on the person against the body, against the spirit, against one's conscience, and against one's convictions. Christ teaches us a special sensitivity for humanity, for the dignity of the human being, for human life, for the human spirit and body. It is this sensitivity that bears witness to knowledge of that "truth which makes us free" (Jn 3:32). It is not permitted for human beings to conceal this truth from themselves. It is not permitted to "falsify" it. It is not permitted to make this truth the object of a "tender." It is necessary to speak of it clearly and simply. And not to "condemn" human beings, but to serve humanity's cause. Liberation also in the social sense begins with knowledge of the truth. (67, p. 1)

Some people are questioning themselves about the mission of the Church today. But cannot the Church of our time catch sight of the truth about her mission in these words of Mary? Do they not contain what we can, what we want to, what we must announce, proclaim, and carry out in this vast field in which "evangelization" and "human advancement" are linked? Does not the Magnificat make it possible to answer the question of knowing what progress, what advancement, is meant, of knowing also what is understood by "evangelizing," proclaiming the Good News to the people of today? For this "today" with its miseries and its signs of hope constitutes, in all countries, a challenge for the "prophetic" mission of the Church, and at the same time for her "motherly" mission. It is a question of opening hearts and mentalities to Christ, to the gospel, to its scale of values, to contribute to the elevation of the whole person and of all persons, to organize a world less unworthy of humanity and of God's plan for humanity, and at the same time, to prepare the kingdom of heaven. (62, p. 3)

Reveals the true meaning of life. Do I then make a mistake when I tell you, Catholic youth, that it is part of your task in the world and the Church to reveal the true meaning of life where hatred, neglect, or selfishness threaten to take over the world? . . . I propose to you the option of love, which is the opposite of escape. If you really accept that love from Christ, it will lead you to God; perhaps in the priesthood or religious life; perhaps in some special service to your brothers and sisters, especially to the needy, the poor, the lonely, the abandoned, those whose rights have been trampled upon, or those whose basic needs have not been provided for. Whatever you make of your life, let it be something that reflects the love of Christ. The whole people of God will be all the richer because of the diversity of your commitments. In whatever you do, remember that Christ is calling you, in one way or another, to the service of love: the love of God and of your neighbor. . . .

Dear young people: Do not be afraid of honest effort and honest work; do not be afraid of the truth. With Christ's help, and through prayer, you can answer his call, resisting temptations and fads and every form of mass manipulation. Open your hearts to the Christ of the Gospels—to his love and his truth and his joy. (120, pp. 268–269)

Evangelization normally involves concern for human development and social progress. You too are attached to your nation's independence and honor; you desire a growth of the means of subsistence, a just order for all, a peaceful life.

You want to serve your country. You are concerned about the poor. And you know that a soulless civilization would not bring happiness. You are ready to devote to this work your labor and your honesty, in respect for all, while banishing hatred, violence, and lying. Those who have responsibility for the common good cannot be unaware that your Christian contribution is beneficial to the country. (152, p. 22)

You who are here . . . are animated by the resolution to collaborate with ever-increasing responsibility in the hierarchical apostolate, in the task of evangelization that belongs to the whole Church. Bear, therefore, effective and concrete witness . . . to the joy of salvation, to the certainty of God's love, which is stronger than all destruction, which can construct on any ruins greater and more beautiful things. Here, then, is the privileged goal, the goal of goals of your work as young Catholics: be apostles of hope and love brought to the world by Christmas. (200, p. 14)

In the pluralistic world that is ours, you have to affirm and cultivate your own religious cultural identity, based on a conception of human beings and of their relationships with truth, which finds its fullness in knowledge of the Word of God, eternal Wisdom, which reveals the ultimate meaning of reality. Take your place more and more in this complete truth, which will enable you to be open to the various cultural values of our world and at the same time to work in it in a way in keeping with what you are. (198, p. 18)

Thinking of the greater good of these kind and generous peoples [the poor], I trust that those in charge, the Catholics and those of good will, . . . will commit their best energies and expand the frontiers of their creativity to build up a more human, and at the same time a more Christian, world. This is the call that the Pope makes to you. (45, p. 8)

And integrates faith and culture. I know that you grasp and are ready to assume the task that awaits you as Christians. You must create within you and around you wide spaces of humanity, spaces to accept and bring to maturity a wisdom about humanity that will illuminate your university studies today and have an impact on your professional service tomorrow. The university seems to me a particularly suitable place to discover and accept consistently your vocation as Christians who live in the world and feel responsible for the world. The task of university students is a great one: it cannot be reduced to the necessity of accumulating knowledge of different sectors in the various fields of learning. There awaits you the task, the effort, of integrating incomplete truths with supreme Truth, freedom with moral responsibility, in the strong unity of Christian life. (229, p. 2)

Your typical function as teachers puts you, as we have mentioned, in a delicate and very special position with regard to the problem, such a relevant one today, of the relations between faith and culture, on which the Fathers of Vatican II drew up some pages, which are among the most sensitive and timely ones, of the pastoral constitution *Gaudium et Spes* (cf. nos. 53–62).

Modern people feel responsible for the progress of culture; they anxiously feel the many contradictions that they must solve. And Christians have the duty of collaborating with everyone for the building of a more human world; culture must be developed in such a way as to perfect the human being in integrity and to help people in carrying out those tasks to which all, but especially Christians, are called.

It is you Catholic teachers who in particular must nourish and adequately prepare in your pupils, with your teaching and your example, that humus, that climate, that inner attitude, in which faith can flourish and develop in its integrity. Through your cultural preparation, show the young how the problem of religious formation cannot be dissociated from that of cultural and human formation; how there exist many fruitful relations between the Christian message of salvation and culture; how the Church, living in the course of the centuries in different conditions, has used the various cultures, the fruit of the genius of several peoples, to spread and explain the Christian message, to study it, to express it in liturgical life and in the varied history of the several communities of faithful; how the gospel of Christ continually renews the life and culture of fallen humanity, opposes and removes errors and evils, purifies and elevates the morality of peoples (cf. Constitution *Gaudium et Spes,* no. 58). (225, p. 8)

If humankind wants to get hold of a revolution that is getting out of hand, if humankind wants to overcome the temptation of the wave of materialism that gains ground as if in flight, if it wants to ensure true development of individuals and peoples, then it must revise in a radical form the concept of progress that under various names has left spiritual values behind. (60, p. 557)

Faithful Christians are also good citizens. Genuine and faithful Christians are also genuine and good citizens. Christians—in any country of the world—are faithful to God, but they also have a deep sense of duty and of love toward their native land and their own people. They respect the things of the spirit and at the same time they consecrate their talents and skills to the common good. (218, p. 614)

In all of you I see the builders of . . . today and tomorrow. . . . You are likewise called to construct the future of your country, a future of peace, prosperity, and concord. That future will be guaranteed only when all citizens, in accordance with their responsibilities and with a single common concern, will be able to create and maintain social relations based on respect for the common good that puts human beings, God's creation, in the center of all things. . . .

All people are builders of the society in which they live. (169, p. 125)

I am happy to know not only that they [Catholics of Bulgaria] remain faithful in their Church, but also that they are setting an example in carrying out their duties as citizens and that they are making an effective contribution to the development of the nation to which they are proud to belong. This is, in my eyes, a natural consequence of the rich spiritual and cultural heritage handed down to the Bulgarian people. . . . It has been possible to show that the Christian faith and culture, far from being alien or in opposition to each other, enrich each other. (28, p. 2)

Whatever their life situation and profession—work, study, sport, community service, farming. People who work enjoy a God-given dignity. God could have created everything on earth in its final form, but he decided differently. For God wants us to be associated with him in the improvement of the things he has made. By our work we share in God's own creative activity. It was the same with Christ himself in his human nature. . . . Work is also a person's way of helping his or her neighbor. One person's work affects another person, and together workers help to build up the whole of society. Those who work can say: "When we work conscientiously, we make a real contribution toward a better world. Our work is an act of solidarity with our brothers and sisters." All who work, whether they are single or married, well-skilled or not, have important rights and responsibilities. For example, each one has the right to proper pay and to reasonable working hours, including time for holidays. And work should never hinder the exercise of one's religious freedom. Work is for the person, not the person for work. So work must not be allowed to dehumanize the person who does the work. (262, p. 596)

Be witnesses to the truth. You seek it in your studies and in the discipline they impose. May they contribute to making your intellectual development as wide as possible and give you the sense of the complexity not only of physical but also of human reality, the capacity and the determination not to stop at too-simple positions. Deepen also, as I have just said, your identity as young Catholic intellectuals. One of the tasks that fall upon you is to overcome, in thought and in action, the dichotomy between theocentrism and anthropocentrism. (207, p. 10)

Every kind of sport brings with it a rich heritage of values that must always be kept in mind in order to be practiced: training in reflection, the correct use of one's energies, the education of the will, the control of sensitivity, methodical preparation, perseverance, resistance, the endurance of fatigue and discomfort, mastery of one's faculties, the sense of loyalty, the acceptance of rules, the spirit of sacrifice and solidarity, faithfulness to commitments, generosity toward the defeated, serenity in defeat, patience with everyone . . . these are a set of moral realities that demand a real, ascetical theology and are a valuable contribution to forming the person and the Christian. (199, p. 17)

Well, know how to unite with the exercise of human virtues, characteristic of your future profession, the noble and ennobling ideal that makes you see Christ himself in your brother and sister in danger or in need (Mt 25:31–46).

I also hope that on returning to your homes at the end of your training, you will be able to fulfill all these good intentions of yours in private and public life: in the formation of your future family, of which you already dream, and in your integration into society as worthy, upright citizens, lovers of progress, justice, peace, and mutual respect. (16, p. 12)

Precisely, you are the Church, Christ living in the rural world. This social framework marks you, and you have the mission to make it more worthy of God and therefore more human. (153, p. 23)

This closeness to nature, this spontaneous awareness of creation as a gift from God, as well as the blessing of a close-knit family—characteristics of farm life in every age including our own—these were part of the life of Jesus. Therefore, I invite you to let your attitudes always be the same as those of Christ Jesus. (124, p. 293)

But they are also there as a presence of Christ. Be faithful to Christ and joyfully embrace his gospel of salvation. Do not be tempted by ideologies that preach only material values or purely temporal ideas; that separate political, social, and economic development from the things of the spirit; and in which happiness is sought apart from Christ. The road toward your total liberation is not the way of violence, class struggle, or hate; it is the way of love, community, and peaceful solidarity. I know that you understand me . . . for you are blessed and possess the kingdom of heaven. (216, p. 616)

Christians, formed by them [Christian churches], will bring to these human solutions a dimension that will enlighten the choice of goals and methods. They will, for example, be concerned about the small and the weak. Their honesty will not tolerate corruption. They will seek more just structures in the landed area. They will provide assistance, solidarity. They will seek to preserve in their community a brotherly and sisterly countenance. They will be artisans of peace. They will consider themselves managers of God's creation, which cannot be wasted or ravaged at will, for it is entrusted to human beings for the good of all. They will avoid the establishment of a materialism that would in fact be a slavery. In short, they want to work, from now on, for a world more worthy of the children of God. That is the role of lay Christians, helped by their pastors. (153, p. 23)

Our times need a witness that expresses openly the will to bring nations and regimes closer to one another, as an indispensible condition for peace in the world. Our times require us not to shut ourselves up in the rigid frontiers of systems but to seek all that is necessary for the good of human beings, who must find everywhere the awareness and certainty of their authentic citizenship. I should say: in whatever system of relationships and forces. (110, p. 95)

For 1979 I know you have chosen the slogan "Hi, we're here too." This motto, even if expressed in a friendly, joking form, sums up well the reason for your activity, which wishes to be first and foremost a Christian presence and evangelical testimony in the midst of the environment in which you live. Remember, however, that if you want this presence to be effective and fruitful, you must undertake to get to know Christ better and better, and to draw from him, who is a great friend of children, the strength to be really, not just in desire, the salt of the earth and the light of the modern world (cf. Mt 5:13–14). . . .

Drawing inspiration from the Christian concept of life and relations among people, you do not wish to let yourselves be prisoners of the merely individualistic logic of profit and gain, but wish to put into practice the teaching of the Second Vatican Council. (31, p. 4)

Reach Peace, Teach Peace!

Peace has become a major preoccupation. Today peace has become, throughout the world, a preoccupation not only for those responsible for the destiny of nations but even more so for broad sections of the population and innumerable individuals who generously and tenaciously dedicate themselves to creating an outlook of peace and to establishing genuine peace between peoples and nations. This is comforting. But there is no hiding the fact that in spite of the efforts of all men and women of good will, there are still serious threats to peace in the world. Some of these threats take the form of divisions within various nations; others stem from deep-rooted and acute tensions between opposing nations and blocs within the world community. In reality, the confrontations that we witness today are distinguished from those of past history by certain new characteristics. In the first place they are worldwide: even a local conflict is often an expression of tensions originating elsewhere in the world. In the same way, it often happens that a conflict has profound effects far from where it broke out. Another characteristic is totality: present-day tensions mobilize all the forces of the nations involved; moreover, selfish monopolization and even hostility are to be found today as much in the way economic life is run and in the technological application of science as in the way that the mass media or military resources are utilized. (252, p. 474)

It can be asked, . . . does the cause of peace among people progress or stagnate? And the answer becomes anxious and uncertain when the persistence of virulent tensions is discovered in many countries, tensions that often give rise to angry outbursts of violence.

Peace, unfortunately, remains rather precarious, while it is easy to have an inkling of the basic motives that are there to threaten it. Where there is no justice—who does not know it—there cannot be peace, because injustice is already a disorder and the word of the prophet always remains true: "Opus justitia pax" (the work of justice is peace, Is 32:17). Likewise, where there is no respect for human rights—I speak of inalienable rights, inherent in the person as person—there cannot be peace, because every violation of personal dignity favors rancor and the spirit of vendetta. And further, where there is no moral formation that favors the good, there cannot be peace, because it is always necessary to watch out for and contain the damaging tendencies that are concealed in the heart. (30, p. 451)

We see that individuals and groups never bring to a conclusion the settling of their secret or public conflicts. Is peace therefore an ideal beyond our grasp? The daily spectacle of war, tension, and division sows doubt and discouragement. In places, the flames of discord and hatred even seem to be kindled artificially by some who do not have to pay the cost. And too often, gestures of peace are ridiculously incapable of changing the course of events, even if they are not actually swept away in the end, taken over by the overbearing logic of exploitation and violence.

In one place, timidity and the difficulty of carrying out needed reforms poison relations between human groups in spite of their being united by a long or exemplary common history; new desires for power suggest recourse to the overpowering influence of sheer numbers or to brute force, in order to disentangle the situation, and this under the impotent and sometimes self-interested and compliant gaze of other countries, near or far; both the strongest and the weakest no longer place confidence in the patient procedures of peace.

Elsewhere, fear of a precarious peace, military and political imperatives, and economic and commercial interests lead to the establishment of arms stockpiles or to the sale of weapons capable of appalling destruction. The arms race, then, prevails over the great tasks of peace, which ought to unite peoples in new solidarity; it fosters sporadic but murderous conflicts and builds up the gravest threats. It is true that at first sight the cause of peace seems to be handicapped to a crippling extent. (37, p. 456)

But we must reach peace. Peace, as I said earlier, is threatened when uncertainty, doubt, and suspicion reign, and violence makes good use of this. Do we really want peace? Then we must dig deep within ourselves, and going beyond the divisions we find within us and between us, we must find the areas in which we can strengthen our conviction that human beings' basic driving forces and the recognition of their real nature carry them toward openness to others, mutual respect, community, and peace. The course of this laborious search for the objective and universal truth about humanity, and the result of the search, will develop men and women of peace and dialogue, people who draw both strength and humility from a truth that they realize they must serve and not make use of for partisan interests. (137, p. 459)

While the advancement of peace in a sense depends on information and research, it rests above all on the action that people take in its favor. Some forms of action envisaged here have only an indirect relationship with peace. However, it would be wrong to think of them as unimportant: as we shall briefly indicate through some examples, almost every section of human activity offers unexpected occasions for advancing peace. Such is the case of cultural exchanges in the broadest sense. Anything that enables people to get to know each other better through artistic activity breaks down barriers. Where speech is unavailing and diplomacy is an uncertain aid, music, painting, drama, and sport can bring people closer together. The same holds for scientific research: science, like art, creates and brings together a universal society that gathers all who love truth and beauty, without division. Thus, science and art are, each at its own level, an anticipation of the emergence of a universal peaceful society. Even economic life should bring people closer together by making them aware of the extent to which they are interdependent and complementary. Undoubtedly, economic relationships often create a field of pitiless confrontation, merciless competition, and even sometimes shameless exploitation. But could not these relationships become instead relationships of service and solidarity and thereby defuse one of the most frequent causes of discord? (252, p. 476)

Christian optimism based on the glorious cross of Christ and on the outpouring of the Holy Spirit is no excuse for self-deception. For Christians, peace on earth is always a challenge because of the presence of sin in the human heart. Motivated by their faith and hope, Christians therefore apply themselves to promoting a more just society; they fight hunger, deprivation, and disease; they are concerned about what happens to migrants, prisoners, and outcasts (cf. Mt 25:35–36). But they know that while all these undertakings express something of the mercy and perfection of God (cf. Lk 6:36, Mt 4:48), they are always limited in their range, precarious in their results, and ambiguous in their inspiration. Only God the giver of life, when he unites all things in Christ (cf. Eph 1:10), will fulfill our ardent hope by himself bringing to accomplishment everything that he has undertaken in history according to his Spirit in the matter of justice and peace. Although Christians put all their best energies into preventing war or stopping it, they do not deceive themselves about their ability to cause peace to triumph, nor about the effect of their efforts to this end. They therefore concern themselves with all human initiatives in favor of peace and very often take part in them. But they regard them with realism and humility. One could almost say that they relativize them in two senses: they relate them both to the self-deception of humanity and to God's saving plan. (252, p. 477–478)

The true spirit of peace must make itself felt in particular at the level of the political leaders and of the groups or centers that control, more or less directly, more or less secretly, the decisive steps either toward peace or toward the prolonging of wars or situations of violence. At the least, people must agree to place their trust in a few elementary but firm principles, such as the following: Human affairs must be dealt with humanely, not with violence. Tensions, rivalries, and conflicts must be settled by reasonable negotiations and not by force. Opposing ideologies must confront each other in a climate of dialogue and free discussion. The legitimate interests of particular groups must also take into account the legitimate interests of the other groups involved and of the demands of the higher common good. Recourse to arms cannot be considered the right means for settling conflicts. The inalienable human rights must be safeguarded in every circumstance. It is not permissible to kill in order to impose a solution. (37, p. 456)

Through concrete and specific efforts. The Church supports and encourages all serious efforts for peace. She unhesitatingly proclaims that the activity of all those who devote the best of their energies to peace forms part of God's plan of salvation in Jesus Christ. But she reminds Christians that they have still greater reasons for being active witnesses of God's gift of peace. In the first place, Christ's word and example have given rise to new attitudes in favor of peace. Christ has taken the ethics of peace far beyond the ordinary attitudes of justice and understanding. At the beginning of his ministry he proclaimed: "Blessed are the peacemakers, for they shall be called children of God" (Mt 5:9).

Those who accept the faith form in the Church a prophetic community: with the Holy Spirit communicated by Christ, after the baptism that makes them part of the body of Christ, they experienced the peace given by God in the sacrament of reconciliation and in eucharistic communion; they proclaim "The Gospel of Peace" (Eph 6:15); they try to live it from day to day, in actual practice; and they long for the time of reconciliation, when by a new intervention of the living God who raises the dead, we shall be wholly open to God and our brothers and sisters. Such is the vision of faith that supports the activity of Christians on behalf of peace. (252, p. 477)

To the lay people who are at present exercising their mission or practicing their profession . . . I also offer my warm good wishes, encouraging them to put into operation, to the extent of their responsibilities, the ideals without which our world could not live in peace: the development of goods and other resources, their distribution, the establishment of just relations, the safeguarding of human rights, the advancement and necessary solidarity between peoples. (140, p. 576)

Today you will contribute to education for peace by highlighting as much as possible the great peacemaking tasks that fall to the human family. In your endeavors to reach a rational and interdependent management of humanity's common environment and heritage, to eradicate the misery crushing millions of human beings, and to strengthen institutions capable of expressing and increasing the unity of the human family on the regional and world level, all will discover the captivating appeal of peace, which means reconciliation of human beings with each other and with their natural universe. By encouraging, in spite of all the current forms of demagogy, the search for simpler ways of life that are less exposed to the tyrannical pressures of the instincts of possessing, consuming, and dominating and more open to the deep rhythms of personal creativity and friendship, you will open up for yourselves and for everyone immense room for the unsuspected possibilities of peace. (37, p. 457)

We must offer to the world visions of peace. What is set free by visions of peace and served by a language of peace must be expressed in gestures of peace. Without such gestures, budding convictions vanish, and the language of peace becomes a quickly discredited rhetoric. The builders of peace can be very numerous if they become aware of their capabilities and responsibilities. It is the practice of peace that leads to peace. The practice of peace teaches those searching for the treasure of peace that the treasure is revealed and presented to those who produce humbly, day by day, all the forms of peace of which they are capable as parents, educators, and young children.

Parents and educators, help children and young people to experience peace in the thousands of everyday actions that are within their capacity at home, at school, at play, with their friends, in team work, in competitive sport, and in the many ways in which friendship has to be established and restored. . . .

Young people, be builders of peace. You are workers with a full share in producing this great common construction. Resist the easy ways out that lull you into sad mediocrity; resist the sterile violence in which adults who are not at peace with themselves sometimes want to make use of you. Follow the paths suggested by your sense of free giving, of joy at being alive, and of sharing. You like to utilize your fresh energies—unconfined by a priori discriminations—in meeting others as brothers and sisters without regard for frontiers, in learning foreign languages to facilitate communication, and in giving disinterested service to the countries with least resources. You are the first victims of war, which breaks your ardor. You are the hope of peace, partners in social endeavors.

Participants in professional and social life, for you peace is often hard to achieve. There is no peace without justice and freedom, without a courageous commitment to promote both. (37, p. 458)

Peace! As the fruit of fundamental order; as the expression of respect for every human being's right to truth, freedom, justice, and love.

Peace of consciences and peace of hearts: this peace cannot be had unless each one of us has the awareness of doing everything in his or her power so that a life worthy of the children of God will be ensured for all men and women, brothers and sisters of Christ, loved by him even to death. I am thinking at this moment in particular of all those who are suffering for the lack of what is strictly necessary for existence, and above all, of little children, who—in their weakness—are the ones who are specially loved by Christ. . . .

May the Risen Christ inspire in all, Christians and non-Christians, sentiments of solidarity and of generous love toward all our brothers and sisters in need. . . .

Christ Jesus himself is the cornerstone of our whole edifice (Eph 2:20–21). . . . and is placed at the very foundation of our faith, hope, and our love. It is the primary reason of our vocation and of the mission that each one of us receives at baptism. (94, p. 721–722)

CHAPTER 3

THE RELATIONSHIP BETWEEN LAITY AND HIERARCHY

Strengthen your Christian and Catholic identity continually.

All have a common call to follow Christ and have rights and duties in the Church and must maintain a Catholic identity in union and communion with the Church.

Every parish is the fundamental community of the People of God.

The parish remains a privileged place where laity live out their community vocation, find support and education in faith, and live out their commitment to others.

Lay groups as organic communities to better serve the Church.

We are witnessing the growth of group forms of lay commitment that become schools of formation and social involvement. These groups must be priestly, prophetic, and royal and should be complementary to each other. When these groups live in union with the hierarchy they become signs of hope for the Church. All such groups should be characterized by their "ecclesiality" and strengthened by good leadership.

Strengthen Your Christian and Catholic Identity Continually

All have a common call to follow Christ. What is holiness? It is precisely the joy of doing God's will. The joy is experienced by human beings by means of constant action upon themselves, by means of faithfulness to Divine law, to the commandments of the gospel, and also not without sacrifices.

The joy is shared by each person always and exclusively thanks to Jesus Christ, the Lamb of God. How eloquent is the fact that we listen to the words spoken by John at the Jordan, when we must prepare to receive Christ in our hearts with Eucharistic Communion! There comes to us He who brings the joy of doing God's will, He who brings holiness.

The parish, as a living particle of the Church, is the community in which we constantly listen to the words "Behold the Lamb of God, who takes away the sin of the world." And we constantly feel the call to holiness. The parish is the community whose main purpose is to make that common call to holiness that comes to us in Jesus Christ, the way for one and all, the way of our whole life—and at the same time of every day. (208, p. 2)

Each member of the Church has an irreplaceable role in it. Yours [priests] also consists in helping all those who belong to your communities to fill theirs, brothers, sisters, laity. You have especially to bring to fulfillment that of the laity: It must never be forgotten, indeed, that baptism and confirmation confer a specific responsibility in the Church. I therefore enthusiastically approve your concern to raise up collaborators, to form them to their responsibilities. Yes, it is necessary to know how to tirelessly address direct, concrete, precise appeals to them. It is necessary to form them by making them aware of the hidden riches that they bear in themselves. It is necessary, finally, to really know how to collaborate, without monopolizing all the tasks, all the initiatives, or all the decisions, when it concerns what is in the area of their competence and their responsibility. (151, p. 11)

And have rights and duties in the Church. Laity look to their pastors above all for food for their faith, assurance in regard to Christ's teachings and the Church's, spiritual sustenance for their lives, and firm orientation for their action as Christians in the world. They also expect rightful room for liberty in their commitment in the temporal order. They expect support and stimulus for the laity without danger of clericalization. Very numerous laity give themselves to the service of the Church . . . with ever greater commitment and unreservedly. May they find in you all that they need for even better service. (170, p. 135)

Therefore, obedience to the teaching of the Second Vatican Council is obedience to the Holy Spirit, who is given to the Church in order to remind her at every stage of history of everything that Christ said, in order to teach the Church all things (cf. Jn 14:26). Obedience to the Holy Spirit is expressed in the authentic carrying out of the tasks indicated by the council, in full accordance with the teaching set forth therein. . . .

The freedom of each individual creates duties, demands full respect for the hierarchy of values, and is potentially directed to the good without limits, to God. In Christ's eyes, freedom is not first of all "freedom from" but "freedom for." The full enjoyment of freedom is love, in particular the love through which individuals give themselves. Human beings, in fact, as we read in the same chapter of *Gaudium et Spes,* "cannot fully find themselves except through a sincere gift of themselves" (no. 24).

It is this interpretation and this exercise of freedom that must be present at the basis of the whole work of renewal. Only the individual who understands and exercises his or her freedom in the manner indicated by Christ opens his or her spirit to the working of the Holy Spirit, who is the Spirit of truth and love. On the authentic affirmation of the freedom of the children of God depends the great work of vocations, to the priesthood, the religious life, marriage. On it also depends effective ecumenical progress and the whole of Christian witness, that is to say, the sharing of Christians in the cause of making the world more human. This is the first condition. (133, pp. 357–358)

And must maintain a Catholic identity. This exalting and demanding mission requires the members of your movements to strengthen their Christian and Catholic identity continually, without which they could not be the witnesses of whom we have spoken. . . .

You cannot strengthen your Catholic identity without strengthening your membership of the people of God in its practical implications. That means being aware that our whole Christian being comes to us through the Church—faith, divine life, sacraments, life of prayer; that the centuries-old experience of the Church nourishes us and helps us to walk along ways that are partly new; that the magisterium is given to the Church to guarantee her authenticity, her unity, and her consistent and safe operation. Even more than that, I hope that your laity will learn to love the Church as a mother, to be happy and proud to be her children and active members. (159, p. 5)

In the community of the faithful—which must always maintain Catholic unity with the bishops and the Apostolic See—there are great insights of faith. The Holy Spirit is active in enlightening the minds of the faithful with this truth and in inflaming their hearts with his love. But these insights of faith and this *sensus fidelium* are not independent of the magisterium of the Church, which is an instrument of the same Holy Spirit and is assisted by him.

It is only when the faithful have been nourished by the word of God, faithfully transmitted in its purity and integrity, that their own charisms are fully operative and fruitful. Once the word of God is faithfully proclaimed to the community and is accepted, it brings forth fruits of justice and holiness of life in abundance.

But the dynamism of the community in understanding and living the word of God depends on its receiving intact the *depositum fidei,* and for this precise purpose a special apostolic and pastoral charism has been given to the Church. It is one and the same Spirit of truth who directs the hearts of the faithful and who guarantees the magisterium of the pastors of the flock. (125, p. 290)

True charisms come from one source. To discern them, St. Paul indicates another criterion, that of unity. This variety of charisms must not generate anarchy, as if it were a question of proud manifestations of human instinct; on the contrary, true charisms are directed to strengthening and enriching unity. . . . In the Christian community the variety of gifts received must be put into the service of the building up of the one Body of Christ and the harmonious development of its vitality. (209, p. 19)

In union and communion with the Church. The Church is essentially a mystery of communion: I would say that it is a call to communion, to life in communion. In vertical communion, let us say, and in horizontal communion: in communion with God himself, with Christ, and in communion with others. It is communion that explains a full relationship between one person and another. The Church is essentially a mystery of communion: intimate communion, always renewed with the very source of life that is the Most Holy Trinity. It is communion of life, of love, of imitation, of following Christ, the Redeemer of humanity, who integrates us closely with God. Hence springs the active, authentic communion of love among us by virtue of our ontological assimilation to him.

A call to communion: live with generous impulse the demands that spring from this reality. Try, therefore, to create unity in thoughts, in sentiments, in initiatives around your parish priests and with them around the bishop, who is the "visible principle and foundation of unity in the particular Church" (cf. Dogmatic Constitution *Lumen Gentium,* no. 23). By means of communion with your bishop, you can reach the certainty of being in communion with the Pope, with the whole Church. (85, p. 6)

Communion between bishops, clergy, and religious constructs communion with the laity. The latter, with all their riches of gifts and aspirations, capacity and initiatives, have a decisive task in the work of evangelizing the modern world. There may legitimately exist in the Church various degrees of connection with the hierarchical apostolate and multiple forms of commitment in the pastoral field. From cordial acceptance of all the forms of clearly Catholic inspiration and from their utilization in plans of pastoral action, there cannot but derive an unquestionable advantage for a more and more incisive presence of the Church in the world. (44, p. 9)

Assembled in the charity of Christ, we are all one in his sacrifice:

• The cardinal archbishop [of Philadelphia] who is called to lead this Church in the path of truth and love

• His auxiliary bishops and the diocesan and religious clergy, who share with bishops in the preaching of the word

• Men and women religious, who through the consecration of their lives show the world what it means to be faithful to the message of the Beatitudes

• Fathers and mothers, with their great mission of building up the Church in love

• Every category of the laity with their particular task in the Church's mission of evangelization and salvation (123, p. 308)

You are also members of the local church communities. These strengthen your commitment to Christ and imbue you with the same Christian spirit that has been in the past the hallmark of . . . Christian communities in various countries of the world. Famous people . . . have encountered Christ and have become Christians through the contact they had with those fervent and dynamic communities. If you maintain that spirit, if you live inspired by the Christian faith . . . you will in a profound way be truly Christian . . . and contribute to the richness of the whole Church. (218, p. 613)

I am certain that there will be a new fervor in Catholic life if every care and attention are made in promoting the apostolate of the laity in the areas that belong to it and according to the forms that are proper to it without allowing this to become, almost imperceptibly, confused with the apostolate proper to the clergy. (212, p. 579)

Every Parish Is the Fundamental Community of the People of God

The parish remains a privileged place. Every parish is the fundamental community of the people of God, in which Christ is present by means of the bishop and priests who operate in his stead. (13, p. 2)

The parishes remain the privileged places where the laity of all environments and all associations can meet to celebrate the Eucharist, at the Sunday service in particular; for prayer; and for catechetical animation, etc. But it is also important that there should exist, in liaison with the other networks, other centers, on a larger scale, or on the contrary, a smaller one, in order to provide for the specialized needs of the people of God in the fields of education, catechesis, welfare, medical assistance, social advancement, etc. They permit a more direct participation of the laity and better adapted action. (128, p. 5)

Where laity live out their community vocation. But if, as a parish, you are called to form one entity in Christ, you are bound to bear witness in your life to this community vocation. In other words, you must undertake to grow in Christ not only as individuals but also as a parish. Do you want to know how a parish community is formed and how it develops? The community is formed first and foremost round the Word of God. Hence the importance of catechesis, by which people start along the way to a deeper and deeper knowledge of the riches of truth contained in the Scriptures. The community develops, then, in participation in liturgical celebrations, especially in participation in the Eucharist. I know that particular care is given to the liturgy in your parish, and I rejoice at this: it is a sign of vitality, which holds out good hopes.

The community grows and is consolidated, furthermore, thanks to the witness of Christian life, which its members know how to offer. Fundamental in this connection is the attitude of courageous consistency that parents must bring to their family and that members of the various organized groups assume before those who still prove to be resistant to the Christian message. A particular element of community growth is constituted, finally, by charitable commitment toward persons who, for one reason or another, are in need: in your parish there is no lack of poor people, sick persons, and the aged; you also have an institute for the rehabilitation of the handicapped. Occasions, therefore, are numerous and stimulating. They, too, represent as many "calls" with which God knocks at the door of your hearts. May he grant you the generosity necessary to respond with enthusiasm and in adequate ways. (211, p. 7)

Find support and education in faith. You who have formed here a living particle of the Church, that is, your parish, have expressed in a particular way this covenant with God, in which you will wish to persevere with the grace of Jesus Christ.

If someone were to ask you why you did so, you could answer in this way, as the Prophet says today: we wish that he should be our

God and that we should be his people: we want his laws to be written on our hearts.

You are looking for a support for these hearts of yours and for your consciences. You are looking for a support for your families. You want them to be stable, not to break up: you want them to form those living hearths of love by which human beings can warm themselves every day. Persevering in the sacramental marriage bond, you wish to hand down life to your children, and together with life, human and Christian education. (86, p. 3)

It is true that catechesis can be given anywhere, but I wish to stress, in accordance with the desire of very many bishops, that the parish community must continue to be the prime mover and preeminent place for catechesis. Admittedly, in many countries the parish has been, as it were, shaken by the phenomenon of urbanization. Perhaps some have too easily accepted that the parish should be considered old-fashioned, if not doomed to disappear in favor of more pertinent and effective small communities. Whatever one may think, the parish is still a major point of reference for the Christian people, even for the nonpracticing. Accordingly, realism and wisdom demand that we continue along the path aiming to restore to the parish, as needed, more adequate structures and, above all, a new impetus through the increasing integration into it of qualified, responsible, and generous members. . . .

In short, without monopolizing or enforcing uniformity, the parish remains, as I have said, the preeminent place for catechesis. It must rediscover its vocation, which is to be a loving and welcoming family home, where those who have been baptized and confirmed become aware of forming the people of God. In that home, the bread of good doctrine and the eucharistic bread are broken for them in abundance in the setting of one act of worship; from that home they are sent out day by day to their apostolic mission in all the centers of activity of the life of the world. (129, p. 345)

In giving thanks for this gift of preserved life and restored health, I wish at this time to express thanks for yet another thing. In fact, it has been granted me in the course of these three months, dear brothers and sisters, to belong to your community: to the community of the sick who are suffering in this hospital and, as a matter of fact, who constitute in a certain sense a special organism in the Church, in the Mystical Body of Christ. In a special way, according to St. Paul, we can say of them that they fill up in their flesh what is lacking the suffering of Christ . . . (cf. Col 1:24). In the course of these months, it was granted me to belong to this special organism. And for this too I heartily thank you, brothers and sisters, at this moment when I take leave of you and your community. (234, p. 1)

And live out their commitment to others. What does "parish" mean? Parish means Christ's presence among humanity. Parish means a set of persons; it means a community in which and with which Jesus Christ reconfirms the presence of God. The parish is a living part of the People of God. . . .

Evangelization—rightly felt as a primary commitment—occupies the priests, the sisters of the two communities present in the parish, the youthful groups of the catechists; and it is developed not only in the ordinary forms but also by means of new approaches, such as by reading and meditating on the gospel in homes, in the so-called "block groups," in which several families gather together for a moment of reflection and communion.

From this contact with the gospel there springs a concrete commitment of charity toward fellow human beings, both in the many initiatives in favor of the old, the sick, the disinherited, to whom large numbers of young people dedicate themselves, and also in solidarity with the problems of the district. This district, having "exploded" rather chaotically in the last few years, bears the sign of not a few inadequacies as regards primary social services and suffers from the discomforts characteristic of recently formed suburban agglomerations.

A great deal, obviously, has still to be done for the ecclesial community to reach full Christian maturity. What has already been done, however, and the intense pulsation of liturgical life within the walls of your new church, consecrated just over a year ago, hold out good hopes for the future of your parish. Recognizing the work you have carried out in the last few years, the Pope wishes to encourage you to persevere with renewed impetus in your Christian testimony within the district. You must feel the responsibility and pride of being leaven in it (cf. Mt 13:33), in order to stimulate opening to Christ and, at the same time, human elevation, thus contributing to the establishment in it of a more just and loving society. (66, p. 3)

Lay Groups as Organic Communities to Better Serve the Church

We are witnessing the growth of group forms of lay commitment. Today, particularly, it is necessary to be able to understand and value lay people who feel the need and almost the anxiety to put themselves in the service of Truth, to proclaim Christ and bear witness to him in the society in which they live.

There exists a deep need for real certainty and true hope; and many lay people feel this necessity and wish to take an active and responsible part in the apostolate, to help bishops and priests. So it is necessary to become aware of this consoling reality and train priests to become conscious of it in their turn so that this enthusiasm, which is a real gift of the Holy Spirit for these times of ours, will not be suffocated and extinguished, or worse, deviated and led astray in mistaken and disappointing experiments.

The gradual revival of the Catholic spirit of association, both through Catholic Action and through recently formed movements, which we all know, is consoling. It is urgent to direct these forces positively, also by means of joint plans, toward an apostolate of presence and precise tasks of evangelization. (243, p. 10)

That spirit [of collaboration] has extended also among the laity, not only strengthening the already-existing organizations for lay apostolate but also creating new ones that often have a different outline and excellent dynamism. Furthermore, lay people have willingly committed themselves to collaborating with the pastors and with representatives of the institutes of consecrated life in the spheres of the diocesan synods and of the pastoral councils in the parishes and dioceses. (73, p. 629)

These groups . . . were formed for the most part of lay Catholics, who found in them, on the one hand, the chance to penetrate into the Council's doctrine, on the other, the chance to express in this regard their own experiences, their own proposals, which showed their love for the Church and their sense of responsibility for the whole of its life in the Archdiocese of Cracow. (107, p. 92)

That become schools of formation and social involvement. Today, I cannot develop these short but exacting reflections that contain the fundamental guiding threads of the life of the associations of Catholic lay people. These associations are schools for the formation of Christians; they encourage them to act like yeast in dough within the People of God, in order to bring forth new vocations in the service of the gospel. In close communion with the Church, they do not isolate themselves in a self-sufficient movement of elites, but they offer a potential of charisms in view of the growth of the People of God in all structures and pastoral activities, under the direction of the bishops.

But Christians must also be the yeast in the dough in the midst of family, social, economic, and political life in the various nations, and also on the international plane, in order to evangelize cultures, in their very roots, in order that there may come about better conditions of peace and justice and the complete development of persons and peoples, so that it will be possible in this way to catch a glimpse of the fruits of community, in common recognition of being children of God. Such demanding tasks cannot be assumed unless Christian lay people and associations of the faithful in general bear a vigorous and enthusiastic testimony to Catholic identity, ecclesial communion, the formation of new persons according to the gospel, and concern with evangelization. (180, p. 20)

Your presence here today indicates a great power for good. You come from many different nations and backgrounds. You bring with you vast experiences in the economic, industrial, professional, cultural, and scientific fields. In the solidarity of your association, you find mutual support, reciprocal encouragement, and a shared commitment to work for the common good. To one who observes you with deep interest and keen attention it seems as though you are offering, with sincerity and generosity, your talents, your resources, and your energies to the service of humanity. And to the extent that you pursue this lofty ideal of reaching out to people everywhere, I am certain that you will continue to find satisfaction and human fulfillment. Indeed, in your very act of giving, of assisting, of helping others to help themselves, you will find enrichment for your own lives. In demonstrating ever greater involvement in the cause of humanity, you will appreciate ever more the unsurpassed dignity and grandeur of the human being, as well as the real fragility and vulnerability of humanity. And in your efforts and endeavors for the good of humanity you can be assured of the understanding and esteem of the Catholic Church. (111, p. 3)

These groups must be priestly, prophetic, and royal. Movements in the Church must reflect the mystery of that love from which she was born and is continually being born. The various movements must live the fullness of the life transmitted to human beings as a gift from the Father in Jesus Christ through the Holy Spirit. They must carry out in all possible fullness the priestly, prophetic, and royal mission of Christ, in which the whole People of God shares.

Movements within the Church-People of God express that multiple movement, which is the human response to Revelation, to the gospel:

- The movement toward the living God himself, who drew so near to humanity
- The movement toward one's interior self, one's conscience, and one's heart, which in the encounter with God reveals its depth
- The movement toward others, our brothers and sisters, whom Christ puts along our way in life
- The movement toward the world, which is ceaselessly waiting for "the revelation of the children of God" in it (Rom 8:19)

The substantial dimension of the movement in each of the above-mentioned directions is love: "God's love has been poured into our hearts through the Holy Spirit which has been given to us" (Rom 5:5). (237, p. 1)

And should be complementary to each other. Each movement pursues its aim with its own methods, in its sector or its environment; but it is important, however, to become aware of your complementarity and to establish links between the movements: not just mutual esteem, a dialogue, but a certain concerted action and even real collaboration. You are called to do so in the name of your common faith; in the name of your common membership of the people of God and, more precisely, of the same local Church; in the name of the same essential goals of the apostolate, faced with the same problems with which the Church and society have to deal. Yes, it is salutary to become aware that the specialization of your movements generally makes it possible to grasp in depth one aspect of realities, but that it calls for other complementary forms of apostolate.

Moreover, you can never forget that in addition to your associations there is a whole people of baptized and confirmed persons, "practicing" faithful who, without enrolling in a movement, carry out personally a real Christian apostolate, an ecclesial apostolate, in their families, in their little communities, especially in their parishes, through their example and by dedication to multiple apostolic tasks. How could I fail to mention here the fine service of catechesis to which so many of the laity in France devote part of their heart and their time, and which calls, moreover, for ongoing formation? (159, p. 5)

When these groups live in union with the hierarchy they become signs of hope for the Church. Communities under the direction of the hierarchy: In my Apostolic Exhortation "Catechesis Tradendae" I indicated and suggested some ways and means of catechesis: media of social communication, pilgrimages, traditional missions, Bible circles, charitable groups, prayer groups, groups of Christian reflection. I also recalled meetings of ecclesial grassroots communities, to the extent to which they correspond to the criteria set forth in the Apostolic Exhortation "Evangelii Nuntiandi," that is:

a. That they remain firmly united with the local churches in which they are integrated and with the universal Church, thus avoiding the danger of becoming isolated and then thinking that they are the only authentic Church of Christ
b. That they preserve sincere communion with the pastors whom the Lord has put in charge of the Church and with the magisterium that the Spirit of Christ has entrusted to them
c. That they grow daily in the sense of responsibility, zeal, and missionary dedication
d. That they never think they are the only recipient or the only agent of evangelization, that is, the only depositary of the gospel, but accept the fact that the Church becomes incarnate also in forms that are not theirs
e. That they seek their nourishment in the Word of God without letting themselves be caught up in political polarization or fashionable ideologies
f. That they avoid the temptation of systematic contestation and the hypercritical spirit on the pretext of authenticity and the spirit of collaboration
g. That they show themselves to be universal and not sectarian (148, p. 16)

How could one fail to wish that everywhere in the world Catholic men and women from all walks of life and assuming temporal responsibilities at all levels may be able to unite in apostolic associations, well integrated in parishes and cities, in order to find there the solid Christian formation that they need, in order to help one another and prepare to bear a real apostolic witness, adapted to present needs and animated by the spirit of love, service, and renewal according to the gospel? This local integration calls, of course, for exchanges and concerted action on the diocesan, national, and international plane. . . .

It is one of the essential characteristics of these Catholic action associations that was highlighted by the recent Council: to pursue, "in closer union with the hierarchy, ends properly apostolic . . . the evangelization and sanctification of all people and the Christian formation of individuals and the Christian formation of their conscience, so as to enable them to imbue with the gospel spirit the various social groups and environments" (Decree *Apostolicam Actuositatem*, no. 20).

The Holy See highly appreciates this deep ecclesial sense of the Council and heartily encourages you to maintain it at all levels. (6, p. 4)

All such groups should be characterized by their "ecclesiality."
I would here say a few words about the basic Christian communities.
. . . Such communities constitute a contemporary experiment in Latin America, above all in this country [Brazil]. This experience ought to be followed, assisted, and deepened, if it is to give the fruit all desire without deviating toward ends not proper to it. (170, pp. 133–134)

Among the dimensions of basic Christian communities I believe it appropriate to call to your attention that which more profoundly defines them and without which their identity would disappear: ecclesiality. I stress this ecclesiality because it already explains the designation that, above all in Latin America, these communities have received. Being ecclesial is their original character and their mode of existing and operating. They are formed in organic communities to better serve the Church. And the base to which they refer is of a clearly ecclesial character and not merely sociological or otherwise. . . .

A delicate attention and a serious and courageous effort to maintain the ecclesial dimension of these communities in all its purity are an eminent service that is good for the communities themselves on the one hand and for the Church on the other. To them, because preserving them in their ecclesial identity guarantees their freedom, effectiveness, and survival. To the Church, because communities that live authentically their ecclesial inspiration with dependencies of another order will serve its essential mission of evangelization. (171, p. 140)

It is also urgent to make an effort to restore to full ecclesial communion those movements, organisms, and groups that springing from the desire of generous and consistent adherence to the gospel are not yet in that community perspective that is necessary for action that is more and more aware of the joint responsibility of all the members of the people of God. It will be necessary to create new opportunities for meeting and dialogue in an atmosphere of openness and cordiality, nourished at the table of the Word of God and the eucharistic bread. It will be necessary to resume dialogue patiently and trustfully, when it has been interrupted, without being discouraged by obstacles and rough patches on the way to comprehension and understanding. But that cannot be reached without obedience, due on the part of all the faithful, to the authentic magisterium of the Church, even with regard to questions connected with the doctrine concerning the faith and morality. Harmony between institutional unity and pastoral pluralism is a difficult goal that is never reached once and for all. It depends on the unanimous and constant effort of all ecclesial members and must be sought in the light of the following axiom, which is still relevant today: *In necessariis unitas, in dubiis libertas, in omnibus caritas* (Unity in necessary things, freedom in doubtful things, and charity in all). (44, p. 603)

And strengthened by good leadership. The role of the leader is, in the first place, to give the example of prayer in the leader's life. With confident hope, with careful solicitude, it falls to the leader to ensure that the multiform patrimony of the Church's life of prayer is known and experienced by those who seek spiritual renewal: meditation on the Word of God, since "ignorance of Scripture is ignorance of Christ," as Saint Jerome insisted; openness to the gifts of the Spirit, without exaggerated concentration upon the extraordinary gifts; imitating the example of Jesus himself in ensuring time for prayer alone with God; entering more deeply into the cycle of the Church's liturgical seasons, especially through the Liturgy of the Hours; the appropriate celebration of the sacraments—with very special attention to the sacrament of penance—which effect the new dispensation of grace in accord with Christ's own manifest will; and above all, a love for and growing understanding of the Eucharist as the center of all Christian prayer. . . .

Second, you must be concerned to provide solid food for spiritual nourishment through the breaking of the bread of true doctrine. The love for the revealed Word of God, written under the guidance of the Holy Spirit, is a pledge of your desire to "stand firm in the gospel" preached by the Apostles. (231, p. 5)

CHAPTER 4

THE SPIRITUAL LIFE OF THE LAITY

Christ desires only your happiness.

The Pope shares his hope and prayer, calls for conversion and a spiritual awakening. This implies a spiritual commitment that is extensive and concrete, a true striving for Christian love.

Seek Jesus always!

Let your life be a continual search for the Savior; love him and others in him. For Jesus who died for us is our support and joy. Mary his Mother is our model.

I know how much you esteem the sacraments.

Laity are called to take an active part in the Church's liturgical life, especially in the eucharist. The liturgical year constantly fosters renewal, and ecclesial prayer is a "first" on the way of true conversion.

Accept the whole message of Christ, without reductions for the sake of convenience.

Today we need a strong personal faith, a real sense of the gospel, fortitude, practical humility, and temperance. For others, almsgiving; for self, even play.

It is necessary to possess an enlightened and convinced faith.

All need a solid catechesis strengthened in experience and tested in daily work. This ongoing formation is fostered in the Church community and necessitates clear conscience formation. This enlightened faith is needed particularly by leaders.

Christ Desires Only Your Happiness

The Pope shares his hope and prayer. I have come to assure you that Christ loves you and desires only your happiness! And he wants you to continue to love one another, understand one another, and help one another in your various needs! May goodness and charity reign in you, in your homes, in your organizations, in the schools, in places of work, study, and entertainment. May Christ always reign in your hearts and in your families. May the fruits of the Spirit, that is, love, joy, peace, patience, kindness, faithfulness, gentleness, and self-control (cf. Gal 5:22), be abundant in you all. (246, p. 9)

In the first place, I hope that you will renew personal and community awareness within you: I am a disciple—I want to be a disciple of Christ. . . . I hope that Christ will be with you, and that through you he will be with others: and that the vocation of his true disciples, who must be "the salt of the earth" and the "light of the world," will be fulfilled in this way. (213, p. 2)

Calls for conversion. The true service of the Christian, in fact, is qualified on the basis of the active presence of God's grace in and through the Christian. Peace in the Christian's heart, moreover, is inseparably united with joy, which in Greek (*chara*) is etymologically akin to grace (*charis*). The whole teaching of Jesus, including his cross, has precisely this aim: "That my joy may be in you, and that your joy may be full" (Jn 15:11). When it pours from a Christian heart into others, it brings forth hope, optimism, and impulses of generosity in everyday toil, infecting the whole of society. (91, p. 9)

The call to repentance, to conversion, means a call to interior opening to others. Nothing in the history of the Church and in the history of humanity can replace this call. This call has infinite destinations. It is addressed to every person, and it is addressed to each one for reasons specific to each one. So all must see themselves in the two aspects of the destination of this call. Christ demands of me an opening to the other. But to what other? To the one who is here, at this moment! It is not possible to postpone this call of Christ to an indefinite moment, in which that "qualified" beggar will appear and stretch out his hand.

I must be open to every person, ready to be helpful. Be helpful, how? It is well known that sometimes we can make a present to the other with a single word. But with a single word we can also strike the other painfully, offend and wound the other: we can even kill the other morally. It is necessary, therefore, to accept this call of Christ in those ordinary everyday situations of coexistence and contact where each of us is always the one who can give to others and, at the same time, the one who is able to accept what others can offer us. (88, p. 1)

Penitence in the evangelical sense means, above all, conversion. From this aspect, the passage of the gospel of Ash Wednesday is very significant. Jesus speaks of the carrying out of acts of penitence, known to and practised by his contemporaries, by the people of the Old Covenant. At the same time, however, he criticizes the purely external way in which these acts —charity, fasting, prayer—are carried out: because this way is contrary to the peculiar finality of the acts themselves. The purpose of the acts of penitence is a sincere turning to God to be able to meet him deep down in the human being in the recesses of the heart. . . .

Therefore, the first and principal meaning of penitence is interior, spiritual. The principal effort of penitence consists in "entering oneself," one's deepest being, entering this dimension of one's own humanity in which, in a certain sense, God is waiting for us. The exterior person must, I would say, yield, in each of us, to the interior person and, in a certain sense, make way for that interior person. In current life, people do not live enough on the interior plane. Jesus Christ clearly indicates that also acts of devotion and penitence (such as fasting, charity, prayer), which because of their religious finality are mainly interior, may yield to the current "exteriorism" and can therefore be falsified. Penitence, on the contrary, as turning to God, requires above all that people should reject appearances, succeed in freeing themselves from falsity, and find themselves again in all their interior truth. (71, p. 1)

Evangelization involves a process of purification and interior change that affects our local churches. It means conversion unto salvation: the ecclesial community becoming ever more a community of living faith, a communion of prayer, a center of charity radiating concern for the poor and the sick, the lonely, the abandoned, the handicapped, those with leprosy, those who are weak in faith, those who need support and are looking for someone to show them the love of Christ. (261, p. 586)

And a spiritual awakening. During these few days that have passed since 16 October, I have had the fortune to hear, from the mouths of authoritative persons, words that confirm the spiritual awakening of modern humanity. These words—and that is significant—were spoken mainly by lay people who fill high offices in the political life of various nations and peoples. They spoke often of the needs of the human spirit, which are not inferior to those of the body. At the same time they indicated the Church, in the first place, as capable of satisfying these needs.

Let what I say now be a first, humble reply to everything I have heard: the Church prays, the Church wishes to pray, she wants to be in the service of the most simple, and at the same time splendid, gift of the human spirit, which is realized in prayer. Prayer is, in fact, the first expression of each one's interior truth, the first condition of true freedom of the spirit.

The Church prays and wishes to pray in order to listen to the interior voice of the divine Spirit, so that he himself, in us and with us, may speak with the sighs, too deep for words, of the whole of creation. The Church prays, and wishes to pray, to meet the needs in the depths of each person, who is sometimes so restricted and limited by the conditions and circumstances of everyday life, by everything that is temporary, by weakness, sin, discouragement, and by a life that seems meaningless. Prayer gives a meaning to the whole of life, at every moment, in every circumstance. (7, p. 1)

The lives of the righteous are different from those of others, and their ways are quite different, and so they end up by being a reproof and condemnation for those who do not live righteously, blinded by wickedness, and do not want to know God's secrets.

Christians, in fact, are in the world, but not of the world (cf. Jn 17:16); their lives must necessarily be different from the lives of those who do not have faith. Their behavior, their lifestyle, their way of thinking, making choices, evaluating things and situations are different because they take place in the light of the word of Christ, which is a message of eternal life. (84, p. 10)

This implies a spiritual commitment that is extensive. You, too, be light in your parish, in your city, in your country! Be light, with constant and convinced attendance at Holy Mass on Sundays and feast days; be light, by scrupulously eliminating foul language, blasphemy, the reading of impure papers and magazines, attendance at negative shows; be light with the continual example of your goodness and your fidelity in every place, but especially in the privileged environment of the family, remembering that "the fruit of light consists in all goodness, justice, and truth." (227, p. 2)

The gospel message, which the Church is called upon to make increasingly part of a people's way of thinking and living, enjoins sincere respect and love for those with different social and political views. It teaches us that every other human being is a brother or sister. It is therefore bound to strengthen the family unity between the children of the same homeland and to encourage mutual respect for the rights of others and for the spiritual values that are the foundations of a society's concord and of its moral and social advancement. (27, p. 4)

And concrete. Always be worthy of your Christian tradition. . . . As everyone knows, it is always a question of a very concrete holiness, based on particular attention to the person or, in evangelical terms, on real love of one's neighbor. It is this Christian witness that the person of today and of always needs. Moreover, it is in this way that Christians realize their identity completely. . . . This faith and love must be seen in action: with them the ecclesial community is nourished and grows; with them, too, the best constructive contribution is made to the whole human society. . . . Faith is the root of charity. . . . (196, p. 15–16)

I deeply approve all the efforts your movements are making to encourage a deepening of the faith, thanks to doctrinal reflection on Christ, the Church, humanity redeemed by Christ, and a real spiritual effort. For, in a word, the apostolic dialogue starts from the faith and presupposes a firm Christian identity. That is all the more necessary, as you experience, since your apostolic activity plunges you into a more secularized world, since the questions raised are more delicate, and those who offer to serve in your movements today are, in spite of their great generosity, less assured in their faith, less supported by Christian structures, and more sensitive to ideologies alien to faith. (159, p. 5)

This parable of the talents teaches us to distinguish true fear of God from false fear. True fear of God is not fright, but rather a gift of the Spirit by which one is afraid of offending him, saddening him, and not doing enough to be faithful to his will, while false fear of God is based on lack of confidence in him and on base human calculation. The one who "walks in the ways of the Lord" (Ps 127 [128]:1) has true fear of God, as was manifested in the behavior of the first and second servants, both praised by the Lord with the words "Well done, good and faithful servant; you have been faithful over a little, I will set you over much" (Mt 25:21, 23). (245, p. 1)

Actually, what is important before the Almighty is not so much history with its ebbs and flows but individuals with their experiences and their longing for the divine and the eternal. And you meet these individuals every day along the way of your life. For them your Christian witness may be of edifying help.

I urge you in particular to sanctify Sunday with participation in Holy Mass, which is the meeting with Christ and with the community; if you really want to, you can succeed in doing so! I recommend to you personal and family prayer and an upright conscience in all your behavior: this is what modern society wants from Christ's followers! (223, p. 4)

A true striving for Christian love. Love is the power that gives rise to dialogue in which we listen to each other and learn from each other. Love gives rise, above all, to the dialogue of prayer in which we listen to God's Word, which is alive in the Holy Bible and alive in the life of the Church.

Let love, then, build the bridges across our differences and at times our contrasting positions. Let love for each other and love for the truth be the answer to polarization, when factions are formed because of differing views in matters that relate to faith or to the priorities for action.

No one in the ecclesial community should ever feel alienated or unloved, even when tensions arise in the course of the common efforts to bring the fruits of the gospel to society around us. Our unity as Christians, as Catholics, must always be a unity of love in Jesus Christ our Lord. (126, p. 292)

Encouragement must be given to the lay associations, movements, and groups, whether their aim is the practice of piety, the direct apostolate, charity and relief work, or a Christian presence in temporal matters. They will all accomplish their objectives better and serve the Church better if they give an important place in their internal organization and their method of action to the serious religious training of their members. In this way every association of the faithful in the Church has by definition the duty to educate in the faith.

This makes more evident the role given to the laity in catechesis today, always under the pastoral direction of their bishops, as the propositions left by the synod stressed several times. (129, p. 346)

Thus, mercy becomes an indispensable element for shaping mutual relationships between people, in a spirit of deepest respect for what is human and in a spirit of mutual love. It is impossible to establish this bond between people if they wish to regulate their mutual relationships solely according to the measure of justice. In every sphere of interpersonal relationships justice must, so to speak, be "corrected" to a considerable extent by that love that, as St. Paul proclaims, "is patient and kind" or, in other words, possesses the characteristics of that merciful love that is so much of the essence of the gospel and Christianity.

Let us remember, furthermore, that merciful love also means the cordial tenderness and sensitivity so eloquently spoken of in the parable of the prodigal son and also in the parables of the lost sheep and the lost coin.

Consequently, merciful love is supremely indispensable between those who are closest to one another: between husbands and wives, between parents and children, between friends; and it is indispensable in education and in pastoral work.

Its sphere of action, however, is not limited to this. If Paul VI more than once indicated the "civilization of love" as the goal toward which all efforts in the cultural and social fields as well as in the economic and political fields should tend, it must be added that that this good will never be reached if in our thinking and acting concerning the vast and complex spheres of human society we stop at the criterion of "an eye for an eye, a tooth for a tooth" and do not try to transform it in its essence, by complementing it with another spirit.

Certainly, the Second Vatican Council also leads us in this direction when it speaks repeatedly of the need to make the world more human and says that the realization of this task is precisely the mission of the Church in the modern world. Society can become even more human only if we introduce into the many-sided setting of interpersonal and social relationships not merely justice but also that "merciful love" that constitutes the message of the gospel. (197, p. 414)

Seek Jesus Always!

Let your life be a continual search for the Savior. Let your life be a continual, sincere search for the Savior, without ever tiring, without ever abandoning the undertaking; even though, at a certain moment, darkness should fall on your spirit, temptations beset you, and grief and incomprehension wring in your heart. These are things that are part of life here below; they are inevitable, but they can also do good because they mature our spirit. You must never turn back, however, even if it should seem to you that the light of Christ, "the light of the peoples," is fading; on the contrary, continue to seek with renewed faith and great generosity.

Deepen your knowledge of Jesus, listening to the word of the ministers of the Lord and reading some pages of the gospel. Try to discover where he is and you will be able to gather from everyone some detail that will indicate it to you, that will tell you where he lives. (87, p. 4)

All that I can say to you is summed up in the words, Get to know Christ and make yourselves known to him. He knows each one of you in a particular way. . . .

The knowledge of Christ is a knowledge full of the simple truth about humanity and, above all, full of love. Submit yourselves to this simple and loving knowledge of the Good Shepherd. Be certain that he knows each one of you more than each one of you knows yourself. He knows because he has laid down his life (cf. Jn 15:13). Allow him to find you. (108, p. 94)

Dear young people, you and I and all of us together make up the Church, and we are convinced that only in Christ do we find real love and the fullness of life. And so I invite you today to look to Christ. . . .

And when you wonder about your role in the future of the world and of the United States, look to Christ. Only in Christ will you fulfill your potential as an American citizen and as a citizen of the world community. (122, p. 296)

So I repeat to you: look for Jesus, by reading and studying the gospel, by reading some good books; look for Jesus by taking advantage in particular of the religious instruction lesson at school, of the catechisms, and of the meetings in your parishes.

To look for Jesus personally, with the eagerness and joy of discovering the truth, gives deep inner satisfaction and great spiritual strength in order then to put into practice what he demands, even though it costs sacrifice. (11, p. 1)

Love him and others in him. Love Jesus present in the Eucharist. He is present in a sacrificial way in Holy Mass, which renews the sacrifice of the cross. To go to Mass means going to Calvary to meet him, our Redeemer.

He comes to us in Holy Communion and remains present in the tabernacles of our churches, for he is our friend; he is everyone's friend and wishes particularly to be the friend and prop of you boys and girls on your way through life; you need confidence and friendship so much.

Love Jesus present in the Church by means of his priests; present in the family by means of your parents and those who love you.

Love Jesus especially in those who are suffering in any way: physically, morally, spiritually; let it be your commitment and program to love your neighbor, discovering Christ's face in him or her. (11, p. 1)

We are his. The Church wants us to look during this whole paschal time to the cross and Resurrection, and to measure our human life with the yardstick of that mystery, which was accomplished on that cross and in that Resurrection.

Christ is the Good Shepherd because he knows human beings; one and all, he knows us with this unique paschal knowledge. He knows us, because he has redeemed us. He knows us, because "he has paid for us": we are redeemed at a high price.

He knows us with the most interior knowledge, with the same knowledge with which he, the Son, knows and embraces the Father, and in the Father, embraces infinite Truth and Love. By means of participation in this Truth and in this Love, he makes us, in himself, once more children of his Eternal Father. He obtains, once and for all, the salvation of humanity, of each person and of all of those that no one shall snatch out of his hand. . . . Who, in fact, could snatch them?

Who can cancel the work of God himself, which the Son has carried on in union with the Father? Who can change the fact that we are redeemed? A fact as powerful and as fundamental as creation itself.

In spite of all the instability of human destiny and the weakness of the human will and heart, the Church orders us today to contemplate the might, the irreversible power of the Redemption, that lives in the heart and hands and feet of the Good Shepherd. Of him who knows us.

We belong once more to the Father because of this love, which did not draw back before the ignominy of the cross, in order to be able to assure all: "No one shall snatch you out of my hand" (cf. Jn 10:28). (147, p. 3)

Jesus, who is present in our suffering neighbor, wishes to be present in every act of charity and service of ours, which is expressed also in every glass of water we give "in his name" (cf. Mk 9:41). Jesus wants love, the solidarity of love, to grow from suffering and around suffering. He wants, that is, the sum of that good which is possible in our human world. A good that never passes away. (63, p. 5)

Christ is heard by the Father:

> Christ of our sufferings,
> Christ of our sacrifices,
> Christ of our Gethsemane,
> Christ of our difficult transformations,
> Christ of our faithful service to our neighbor.
> Christ of our pilgrimages to Lourdes,
> Christ of our community, today, in St. Peter's Basilica.
> Christ our Redeemer,
> Christ our Brother!
> Amen. (63, p. 5)

For Jesus who died for us. Christ "gave up his life for us: and we, too, ought to give up our lives for one another" (1 Jn 3:16). A "new nature" (Col 3:10), a new world marked by filial relationships with God and communal relationships with people, let us say, a new humanity: these are the fruits that we expect from the Bread of Life that the Church breaks and distributes in the name of Christ. Here is something that must be stated: the deepest level at which this link with Christ's Body is realized in communicants, this "osmosis" of Christ's divine love, is higher than human feelings and measures. It belongs to the order of grace, to the mysterious sharing through faith in the life of the Risen Christ, according to the spirit of holiness (cf. Rom 1:4). But normally there should flow from it great moral consequences, those which Saint Paul enumerates in the second part of each of his letters. These consequences are simultaneously demands and invitations, for they presuppose the openness and responsibility of those taking part. What profound implications for the relationships between those who communicate, especially: "The Eucharist makes the Church," it joins together as the members of one body those who share in the same Body of Christ, "that all may be one" (Jn 17:21). And also, what great consequences for society itself, for the manner of bringing people together in communal unity, especially the very poor; of serving them; of sharing with them the bread of the earth and the bread of love; of building up with them a more just world, a world more worthy of the children of God; and at the same time of preparing a new world for the future, in which God himself will bring definitive renewal and total and endless communion (cf. Rev 21:1, 5; cf. Constitution *Gaudium et Spes,* nos. 39, 45). (36, pp. 9–10)

Is our support and joy. Jesus is first of all the support of our suffering. . . .

The Christian knows that, after original sin, human history is always a risk. But the Christian also knows that God himself willed to enter our grief, feel our pangs, pass through the agony of the spirit and the torment of the body. Faith in Christ does not take away suffering, but illuminates it, raises it, purifies it, sublimates it, and makes it efficacious for eternity.

In any pain of ours, moral or physical, let us look at the Crucified! Let the Crucified reign, clearly visible and venerated, in our houses. Only he can comfort and reassure us!

In the second place, Jesus is the foundation of our joy. Christian joy is a reality that is not easy to describe, because it is spiritual and also belongs to the mystery. Those who really believe that Jesus is the Word Incarnate, the Redeemer of all, cannot but feel within themselves a sense of immense joy, which is consolation, peace, abandonment, resignation, bliss.

It is the joy of interior light on the meaning of life and history;

It is the joy of God's presence in the soul, by means of grace;

It is the joy of God's forgiveness, by means of his priests, when one has, unfortunately, offended his infinite love, and having repented, returns to the Father's arms;

It is the joy of the expectation of eternal happiness, as a result of which life is understood as an "exodus," a pilgrimage, committed though we are in the affairs of the world.

To you, too, as to the Apostles, Jesus says: "These things I have spoken to you, that my joy may be in you, and that your joy may be full" (Jn 15:11). "No one will take your joy from you" (Jn 16:22). (81, p. 3)

I know you place your hope in that cross, which has become for us all a "royal banner" (liturgical hymn of Passiontide). Continue to be imbued, every day and in every circumstance, with the wisdom and strength that come to us only from Christ's paschal cross. Try to draw from this experience an ever-new purifying energy. The cross is the pressure point to act as a lever for a service of all people, so as to transmit to so many others the immense joy of being Christians. . . .

My children, only if you have in you this divine grace that is joy and peace will you be able to construct something worthwhile for all people. Consider your university vocation, therefore, in this magnificent Christian perspective. Study today, professional work tomorrow, become for you a way in which to find God and serve others, your brothers and sisters: that is, they become a way of holiness, as beloved Cardinal Albino Luciani said pithily just before he was called to this See of Peter, with the name of John Paul I: "There, right in the very street, in the office, in the factory, one becomes holy, provided one carries out one's duty competently, for love of God and joyfully; in such a way that daily work will not become 'a daily tragedy,' but almost 'a daily smile.' " (91, p. 9)

For God and before God, the human being is always unique and unrepeatable, somebody thought of and chosen from eternity, someone called and identified by his or her own name.

At the same time, the birth of Jesus in Bethlehem gives witness that God has expressed this eternal word in time, in history. With this expression, God has built up and continues to build up the structure of human history. The birth of the Incarnate Word is the beginning of a new power for humanity itself, the power open to every person, in accordance with the words of St. John: "He gave power to become children of God." . . .

Humanity's power resides in this mystery, the power that permeates anything that is human. Do not make it hard for that power to exercise its influence. Do not destroy its influence. Everything that is human grows from this power. Without this power it perishes. Without this power it falls to ruin. (32, pp. 454–455)

We must note that Christ, in revealing the love-mercy of God, at the same time demanded from people that they also should be guided in their lives by love and mercy. This requirement forms part of the very essence of the messianic message and constitutes the heart of the gospel ethos. The Teacher expresses this both through the medium of the commandment that he describes as the greatest and also in the form of a blessing, when in the Sermon on the Mount he proclaims: "Blessed are the merciful, for they shall obtain mercy."(197, p. 404–405)

Mary his mother is our model. [Mary] enables us to overcome the multiple "structures of sin" in which our personal, family, and social life is wrapped. She enables us to obtain the grace of true liberation, with that freedom with which Christ liberated every person.

From here too starts . . . the authentic commitment for others, our brothers and sisters, especially for the poorest and the neediest ones, and for the necessary transformation of society. For this is what God wants from us, and it is to this that he sends us, with the voice and strength of his gospel, making us responsible for one another. . . .

For in this way she [Mary] is "the type of Christ's perfect disciple who is the architect of the earthly and temporal city, but who at the same time aims at the heavenly and eternal city: who promotes justice, liberates the needy, but above all, bears witness to that active love that constructs Christ in souls." (58, p. 3)

Among all the titles given to the Virgin through the centuries for her motherly love for Christians, there is one that stands out: *virgo fidelis* (faithful virgin). But what does this fidelity of Mary mean? What are the dimensions of this fidelity?

The first dimension is searching. Mary was faithful when she searched for the profound meaning of the will of God in her life. . . .

The second dimension of this fidelity is called acceptance, to accept. The *quomodo fiat* is transformed on the lips of Mary as a *fiat* (let it be): let it be, I am willing, I accept. . . .

Coherence is the third dimension of fidelity. To live in accordance with what one believes. To adjust one's life to what one adheres to. . . .

But fidelity must stand the most difficult test: perseverance. That is the fourth dimension of fidelity, perseverance. . . .

The *fiat* of Mary at the annunciation finds its fulfillment in the *fiat* at the foot of the cross. To be faithful is to remain faithful in private to what we proclaimed in public. (50, p. 541)

We too, today, contemplate her to learn, on the basis of her example, how to build the Church. And for that, we know that we must, above all, progress under her direction in the exercise of the faith. Mary lived her faith in an attitude of continual deepening and progressive discovery, passing through difficult and shadowy moments, beginning with the first days of her maternity (cf. Mt 1:8ff): moments that she overcame, thanks to a responsible attitude of listening and obedience with regard to the word of God. We too must strive to deepen and consolidate our faith by listening, welcome, proclamation, veneration of the word of God, by attentive examination of the signs of the times in its light, through interpretation and fulfillment of the events of history (cf. Paul VI, Apostolic Exhortation *Marialis Cultus,* no. 17).

Mary is presented to us as an example of courageous hope and of active charity: she made her way in hope with docile promptness, in passing from Jewish hope to Christian hope, and she lived charity, welcoming its demands even to the most total gift and to the greatest sacrifice. Faithful to her example, we too must remain firm in hope, even when storm-laden clouds bank up over the Church, which advances like a ship in the midst of the waves, often unfavorable, of the events of this world. We too must grow in charity, by developing humility, poverty, availability, the capacity for listening and attention, by adhering to what she teaches us by the witness of her whole life. (136, p. 427)

But the task of renewal in Christ is never finished. Every generation, with its own mentality and characteristics, is like a new continent to be won for Christ. The Church must constantly look for new ways that will enable her to understand more profoundly and to carry out with renewed vigor the mission received from her founder.

In this arduous task, like so many times before when the Church was faced with a new challenge, we turn to Mary, the mother of God and the seat of wisdom, trusting that she will show us again the way to her Son. (118, p. 327)

From the time when Jesus, dying on the cross, said to John: "Behold your mother"; from the time when "the disciple took her to his own home," the mystery of the spiritual motherhood of Mary has been actualized boundlessly in history. Motherhood means caring for the life of the child. Since Mary is the mother of us all, her care for the life of human beings is universal. The care of a mother embraces her child totally. Mary's motherhood has its beginning in her motherly care for Christ. In Christ, at the foot of the cross, she accepted John, and in John she accepted all of us totally. Mary embraces us all with special solicitude in the Holy Spirit. For as we profess in our Creed, he is "the giver of life." It is he who gives the fullness of life, open towards eternity.

Mary's spiritual motherhood is therefore a sharing in the power of the Holy Spirit, of the giver of life. It is the humble service of her who says of herself: "Behold, I am the handmaid of the Lord" (Lk 1:38). (267, p. 1)

I Know How Much You Esteem the Sacraments

Laity are called to take an active part in the Church's liturgical life. As members of the laity, you are called to take an active part in the sacramental and liturgical life of the Church, especially in the eucharistic sacrifice. At the same time you are called to spread the gospel actively through the practice of charity and through involvement in catechetical and missionary efforts, according to the gifts that each one of you has received (cf. 1 Cor 12:4ff). In every Christian community, whether it be the "domestic church" constituted by the family, or the parish collaborating with the priest, or the diocese united around the bishop, the laity strive, like the followers of Christ in the first century, to remain faithful to the teaching of the apostles, faithful to community service, faithful to prayer and to the celebration of the eucharist (cf. Acts 2:42). (155, p. 47)

Because you believe in Christ and have been regenerated in the sacrament of baptism, you are children of God. Because you believe in Christ you are able to approach him in the sacrament of penance and to receive his love in the Holy Eucharist. I know how much you esteem the sacraments, and I want to encourage you to remain ever faithful to them. They are your source of life and hope, and they will give you strength to remain true to your calling as Christians, real Christians. (219, p. 617)

Baptism, therefore, is truly a new birth, a rebirth, as the Apostle himself expresses it: "The washing of regeneration and renewal in the Holy Spirit" (Ti 3:5). And it is for this reason that all of us, at this time, rejoice with deep spiritual joy. Ours is the joy of the ecclesial family, which corresponds exactly to the joy at the moment of delivery, when the mother exults because "a child is born into the world" (Jn 16:21). This is what we are doing, because at this moment some new members are entering the family of God, and if they acquire in him a new Father, they also find in us new brothers and sisters, ready to welcome them with care and with exultation into the great community of the children of God. (256, p. 2)

Through baptism we are incorporated into the Church. The minister, our parents, and godparents sign us with the sign of the cross, Christ's proud standard. This shows that it is the whole assembly of the faithful, the whole community of Christ, that supports us in the new life of faith and obedience that follows from our baptism, our new birth in Christ.

In baptism we are drawn into the community of faith. We become part of the pilgrim People of God that in all times and in all places goes forward in hope toward the fulfillment of the "promise." It is our task to take our place responsibly and lovingly beside those who from the beginning "remained faithful to the teaching of the apostles, to the community, to the breaking of bread, and to the prayers" (Acts 2:42).

Baptism creates a sacramental bond of unity linking all who have been reborn by means of it. But baptism, of itself, is only a beginning, a point of departure, for it is wholly directed toward the fullness of life in Christ (cf. *Unitatis Redintegratio,* no. 22). Baptism is the foundation of the unity that all Christians have in Christ: a unity we must seek to perfect. When we set out clearly the privilege and the duty of the Christian, we feel ashamed that we have not all been capable of maintaining the full unity of faith and charity that Christ willed for his Church.

We the baptized have work to do together as brothers and sisters in Christ. The world is in need of Jesus Christ and his gospel—the good news that God loves us; that God the Son was born, was crucified, and died to save us; that he rose again and that we rose with him; and that in baptism he has sealed us with the Spirit for the first time, gathered us into a community of love and of witness to this truth. (269, p. 2)

Especially in the Eucharist. Because you believe in Christ and have been regenerated in the sacrament of baptism, you are children of God. Because you believe in Christ you are able to approach him in the sacrament of penance and to receive his love in the Holy Eucharist. I know how much you esteem the sacraments and I want to encourage you to remain ever faithful to them. They are your source of life and hope and they will give you strength to remain true to your calling as Christians, real Christians. (219, p. 617)

Our people have a supernatural sense whereby they look for reverence in all liturgy, especially in what touches the mystery of the Eucharist. With deep faith our people understand that the Eucharist—in the Mass and outside the Mass—is the body and blood of Jesus Christ and therefore deserves the worship that is given to the living God and to him alone. (125, p. 291)

Our full participation in the Eucharist is the real source of the Christian spirit that we wish to see in our personal lives and in all aspects of society. Whether we serve in politics, in the economic, cultural, social, or scientific field—no matter what our occupation is—the Eucharist is a challenge to our daily lives. (116, p. 270)

The liturgical year constantly fosters renewal. Lent must leave a strong and lasting mark on our lives. It must renew in us awareness of our union with Jesus Christ, who makes us see the necessity of conversion and indicates to us the ways to reach it. Prayer, fasting, and almsdeeds are precisely the ways that Christ indicated to us. . . .

First, then, the way of prayer. I say "first," because I wish to speak of it before the others. But saying "first," I want to add today that in the complete work of our conversion, that is, of our spiritual development, prayer is not isolated from the other two ways that the Church defines with the evangelical term of "fasting and almsdeeds." The way of prayer is perhaps more familiar to us. We understand more easily, perhaps, that without it it is not possible to be converted to God, to remain in union with him, in that communion that makes us mature spiritually. (78, p. 2)

The liturgy of Advent has prepared us spiritually to relive the mystery that marked a turning point in human history: the birth of a child who is also the Son of God, the birth of the Savior.

It is an event that really changed the face of the world. Is not the very atmosphere of joy that one breathes along the streets of cities and villages, at places of work, and in the privacy of one's home a testimony of that? The feast of Christmas has entered customs as an undisputed occasion and stimulus for a kind thought, an act of altruism and love. This blossoming of generosity and courtesy, attention and thoughtfulness, puts Christmas among the most beautiful moments of the year, of life, in fact, impressing itself also on those who have no faith and yet are unable to resist the fascination that springs from this magic word: Christmas. (254, p. 3)

Another point I would like to submit to your attention concerns the formation of Christian consciences to a liturgical spirit, in view of a healthy and wise renewal of popular piety.

The reality and importance of popular piety is happily being rediscovered in several quarters. Its significance must not be underestimated. There exists, in fact, the danger of attaching to these expressions of the spirit the merely anthropological or sociological sense of subculture, excluding and ignoring the genuinely religious content, as a result of prejudicial patterns. On the contrary, it is often a question of moments of religious fullness in which human beings recover an identity lost or shattered, by rediscovering their own roots. Support of a certain fashion that depreciates popular piety involves the risk of turning towns and villages into a desert without a history, without a culture, without a religion, without a language, and without an identity, with very serious consequences.

As I said in the homily delivered at the Sanctuary of Our Lady of Zapopan, in Mexico, on 30 January 1979, "This popular piety is not necessarily a vague sentiment, lacking a solid doctrinal basis. . . . How often it is, on the contrary, the real expression of the soul of a people, since it is touched by grace and forged by the happy meeting between the work of evangelization and local culture." (247, p. 4)

And ecclesial prayer is a "first" on the way of true conversion.
Christ himself indicates to us in the gospel the rich program of conversion. Christ—and after him, the Church—also proposes to us in the time of Lent the means that serve for this conversion. It is a question in the first place of prayer, then of almsdeeds and fasting. We must accept these means and introduce them into our lives in proportion to the needs and possibilities of the person and of the Christian of our times. Prayer always remains the first and fundamental condition of approach to God. During Lent we must pray, we must make an effort to pray more, to look for the time and the place to pray. It is prayer in the first place that brings us out of indifference and makes us sensitive to the things of God and of the soul. Prayer also educates our consciences, and Lent is a particularly suitable time to reawaken and educate conscience. Just in this period the Church reminds us of the indispensable necessity of sacramental confession, in order that we all may be able to live the resurrection of Christ not only in the liturgy but also in our own soul. (75, p. 1)

I would like to stress only one thing today. All of us, when we pray, are disciples of Christ, not because we repeat the words that he once taught us, sublime words, the complete content of prayer; we are disciples of Christ even when we do not use these words. We are his disciples only because we pray: "Listen to the Master praying: learn to pray. He prayed, in fact, for this reason, to teach people to pray," St. Augustine affirms (*Enarrationes,* in Ps 56: 5). . . . . To pray means speaking to God—I would venture to say even more—to pray means finding oneself again in that One eternal Word through which the Father speaks, and which speaks to the Father. (78, p. 1)

It is necessary to pray taking this essential concept of prayer as our basis. When the disciples asked the Lord Jesus, "Teach us to pray," he replied with the words of the prayer Our Father, thus creating a concrete model that is at the same time universal. In fact, all that can and must be said to the Father is contained in those seven requests, which we all know by heart. There is such a simplicity in them, and also such a depth, that a whole life can be spent meditating on the meaning of each of them. Is this not so? Does not each of them speak to us, one after the other, of what is essential for our existence, directed completely to God, to the Father? Does it not speak to us of our "daily bread," of "forgiveness of our trespasses as we also forgive them," and at the same time of "preservation from temptation" and "deliverance from evil"?

When, in answer to the request of the disciples "teach us to pray," Christ utters the words of his prayer, he teaches not only the words, but he teaches that in our talk with the Father there must be complete sincerity and full openness. Prayer must embrace everything that is part of our life. It cannot be something additional or marginal. Everything must find in it its true voice: even everything that burdens us, things of which we are ashamed, what by its very nature separates us from God. This above all. It is prayer that always, first of all and essentially, demolishes the barrier that sin and evil may have raised between us and God. (78, p. 2)

Prayer, in fact, despite a beautiful renewal seen here and there, continues to be very difficult for many Christians, who pray little. They ask themselves, Of what value is prayer? Is it compatible with our modern sense of efficiency? Is there not perhaps something wretched in responding with prayer to the material and spiritual needs of the world?

In light of this difficulty we must demonstrate incessantly that Christian prayer is inseparable from our faith in God, Father, Son, and Holy Spirit, from our faith in his love and his redeeming power, which is at work in the world. Therefore, prayer is worthwhile above all for us: Lord, "increase our faith!" (Lk 17:6). It has as its goal our conversion, that is, as St. Cyprian explained, interior and exterior openness, the will to open oneself to the transforming action of grace. "Saying 'May your name be holy,' we ask insistently why we were sanctified with baptism, to persevere in that which we have begun. . . . 'Your kingdom come': we ask that the kingdom of God be realized in us in the sense in which we implore that his name be sanctified in us. . . . We then add, 'May your will be done on earth as it is in heaven,' in order that we may do as God wills. . . . The will of God is that which Christ did and taught" (St. Cyprian, *De Oratione Dominica*). (233, p. 185)

If it is true that revolution is passing through the world, the one you extolled at the beginning of our meeting, then this revolution is the one most necessary for humanity. Disappointed by so many programs, so many ideologies, bound up with the dimension of the body, with transiency, with the order of matter, human beings submit to the action of the Spirit and discover within themselves the desire for what is spiritual. I think that such a revolution is really passing over the world today. There are many communities that pray, pray as perhaps they have never done before, in a different way, a more complete and richer way, with a greater receptiveness for that gift that the Father gives us; and also with a new human expression of this receptiveness; I should say, with a new cultural program of new prayer. Such communities are numerous. I wish to unite with them wherever they may be on Polish soil, and all over the earth.

This great revolution of prayer is the fruit of the gift, and it is also the testimony of the vast needs of modern people and of the threats looming over them and over the modern world. I think that Abraham's prayer (and its content) is very relevant in the times in which we live. Such a prayer is also necessary, to negotiate with God for every just person, to redeem the world from injustice. A prayer that makes its way into God's heart, so to speak, between what is justice and what is mercy in it, is indispensable. (173, p. 5)

Accept the Whole Message of Christ, Without Reductions for the Sake of Convenience

Today we need a strong personal faith. Today, in fact, an enlightened, deep, logically personalized faith is necessary, and this can only be achieved by means of reflection, in order not to let it be disturbed and swept away by the impetuous fury of current opinions, morals, and mentality.

Continue, therefore, to meditate from time to time on the supreme truths revealed by Jesus and taught by the Church, which illuminate our destiny in a unique and determinate way; commit yourselves to being more and more people convinced about the truth of faith! This is what the times require; this is what the Lord demands of each of us in our profession, in our work. (143, p. 11)

But I would also like to leave you a spiritual memory that will serve you as a program of life and as inspiration in your important moments of decision. What can I say to you but what St. Peter wrote to the first Christians: "Resist, . . . firm in your faith!" (cf. 1 Pt 5:9). Yes, my dear children, keep firm your faith in Jesus Christ, as the martyrs of Otranto did!

Keep firm your faith in moments of trial and suffering, remembering that Peter himself wrote, "Rejoice insofar as you share Christ's sufferings, that you may also rejoice and be glad when his glory is revealed. . . . Yet if one suffers as a Christian, let that person not be ashamed, but under that name let the Christian glorify God!" (1 Pt 5:13, 16).

Keep your faith firm, especially in the tumult of history, which envelops us all and sometimes sweeps us along, with its conflicts and its tragic events. In the mysterious dialectics between human freedom and divine grace, between humanity's sin and the Redemption of Christ, we are not alone. I am happy to repeat to you, too, what I said at Le Bourget during my journey to Paris: "The problem of the absence of Christ does not exist. The problem of his moving away from human history does not exist. God's silence with regard to the anxieties of the human heart and the fate of humanity does not exist. There is only one problem that exists always and everywhere: the problem of our presence beside Christ, of our intimacy with the authentic truth of his words and with the power of his love" (Homily of the Mass at Le Bourget, 1 June 1980).

Sometimes the horizon of history darkens, and hearts tremble before the terrible power of hate and violence. Keep firm faith in Jesus: he is our peace and he guides events for the good of those who humbly love God and serve him in their brothers and sisters. "Therefore gird up your minds"—I say to you again with St. Peter—"be sober, set your hope fully upon the grace that is coming to you at the revelation of Jesus Christ. . . . As he who called you is holy, be holy yourselves in all your conduct" (1 Pt 1:13, 15). (183, p. 8)

In these situations, which may cause the temptation of dejection, discouragement, or psychological surrender, I wish to exhort you today, recalling the great Christian tradition of your predecessors, to reaffirm your faith courageously and with commitment; to guard it in your heart; to profess it publicly, without fear or weakness, by word and by example, always in radical consistency with the requirements of the Christian concept, sometimes hard ones. (186, p. 5)

A real sense of the gospel. Keep alive in you and always preserve this youthful sense of the gospel, which the people of today need so much, and bear witness to it in your environment. I would like to tell you that it is in order not to grow old that we must cling tenaciously to Jesus and his proclamation. Only love, in fact, which is the soul of the gospel, enables us to be always young. You know the episodes of violence of our days: how many deaths they cause, and how many tears! Well, the one who causes deaths is not only old, but is already dead inside. Life, in fact, springs only from love and therefore from another life, or from a death faced lovingly, like that of Jesus. So cultivate the most genuine love for everyone, always ready to help those in need, to forgive those who offend you, and even to correct or at least have compassion for those who act tyrannically.

Let these, dear students, be the essential commitments of your lives. And since, as you know, we are now living in the period of Lent, try to put them into practice straightaway as preparation for next Easter. Your happiness will be all the more pure, the more it has passed through trial, sacrifice, and self-mastery. (142, p. 11)

It depends on us, in fact, to gather the meaning brought by Christ to human existence and to "incarnate it" in our lives. It depends on the commitment of all to incarnate this meaning in human history. A great responsibility and a sublime dignity! For this purpose, consistent and courageous witness to our faith is necessary. St. Paul, writing to the Ephesians, draws up a concrete program of life, in this sense:

- It is necessary, first of all, to abandon the wordly and pagan mentality: "Now this I affirm and testify in the Lord, that you must no longer live as the Gentiles do, in the futility of their minds."
- Then, it is necessary to change the worldly and earthly mentality into the mentality of Christ: "Put off your old nature which belongs to your former manner of life and is corrupt through deceitful lusts."
- Finally, it is necessary to accept the whole message of Christ, without reductions for the sake of convenience, and live according to his example: "Be renewed in the spirit of your minds, and put on the new nature, created after the likeness of God in true righteousness and holiness." (Eph 4:17, 20–24)

As you see, dear children, it is a very exacting program; from certain points of view it could even be called a heroic one. Yet we must present it to ourselves and to others in its integrality, relying on the action of grace, which can give all of us the generosity to accept responsibility for our own actions in an eternal perspective and for the good of society.

Go on, therefore, with confidence and generous commitment, seeking new impetus and new joy every day in devotion to Jesus in the Eucharist and in trust in the Virgin Mary.

I am happy to conclude by quoting to you the thought of my revered predecessor Paul VI (in his address to the cardinals, 21 June 1976), the first anniversary of whose pious death falls tomorrow: "In the spate of conflicting interests, harmful to humanity's real good, it is necessary to proclaim again the great words of the gospel, which alone have given all people light and peace in other similar upheavals of history" (cf. *Insegnamenti di Paolo VI*, vol. 4, p. 502).

So, beloved children, with the light and the peace that come to us from these eternal words, we continue serenely on our way. (113, p. 3)

Fortitude. As can be seen from all this, the manifestations of the virtue of fortitude are numerous. Some of them are well known and enjoy a certain fame. Others are less known, although they often call for even greater virtue. Fortitude, in fact, as we said in the beginning, is a virtue, a cardinal virtue. . . .

I wish to pay tribute to all those unknown, courageous people. To all those who have the courage to say "no" or "yes" when they have to pay a price to do so. To those who bear extraordinary witness to human dignity and deep humanity. (15, p. 1)

What, then, is the value of your suffering? You have not suffered or do not suffer in vain. Pain matures you in spirit, purifies you in heart, gives you a real sense of the world and of life, enriches you with goodness, patience, and endurance, and—hearing the Lord's promise re-echo in your heart; "Blessed are those who mourn, for they shall be comforted" (Mt 5:4)—gives you the sensation of deep peace, perfect joy, and happy hope. Succeed, therefore, in giving a Christian value to your suffering, succeed in sanctifying your suffering, with constant and generous trust in him who comforts and gives strength. I want you to know that you are not alone or separated or abandoned in your "Via Crucis"; beside you, each one of you, is the Blessed Virgin, who considers you her most beloved children: Mary, who "is a mother to us in the order of grace . . . from the consent which she loyally gave at the Annunciation and which she sustained without wavering beneath the cross . . ." (Dogmatic Constitution *Lumen Gentium*, nos. 61–62), is close to you because she greatly suffered with Jesus for the salvation of the world. (100, p. 4)

Practical humility. It is true we must be humble, all the more so that dullness, weakness, selfishness, and injustice are also in us. Humble, but never resigned. Never discouraged. Never inactive. The first Christians did not let themselves be stopped by such considerations, even though they seemed lost in the immense Roman Empire, which had other morals. Nor must the modern apostles of charity. For the transformation of the world, which is in God's hands, begins with the conversion of hearts, of the heart of each one, mine and yours. It begins with the way of treating as a neighbor the Samaritan whom I meet on my way today, or whom I am trying to meet. It is a question of establishing the atmosphere of the community willed by Christ, of realizing a concrete part of it, and preparing to assume better your responsibilities as men and women tomorrow. It is a question, in a view of faith, of unifying with Christ the Redeemer these prayers and these acts of love carried out in the Church, and of hoping for the grace of resurrection that will transfigure them. (203, p. 11)

Bowing the head may be interpreted as a gesture of humiliation or resignation. Bowing the head before God is a sign of humility. Humility, however, is not identified with humiliation or resignation. It is not accompanied by faintheartedness. On the contrary, humility is creative submission to the power of truth and love. Humility is rejection of appearances and superficiality; it is the expression of the depth of the human spirit; it is the condition of its greatness.

St. Augustine, too, reminds us of this. In a sermon he says: "Do you want to be a great? Begin from the smallest thing. Do you intend to construct a large building that rises up very high? Take into consideration in the first place the foundation of humility" (St. Augustine, *Sermon* 69.2, in *PL* 38:441). (77, p. 2)

And temperance. The virtue of temperance guarantees every person mastery of the "lower self" by the "higher self." Is this a humiliation of our body? Or a disability? On the contrary, this mastery gives higher value to the body. As a result of the virtue of temperance, the body and our senses find the right place that pertains to them in our human condition.

A temperate person is one who is master of himself or herself, one in whom passions do not prevail over reason, will, and even the "heart": a person who can control himself or herself! If this is so, we can easily realize what a fundamental and radical value the virtue of temperance has. It is even indispensable, in order that a person may be fully a person. (17, p. 2)

We sometimes hear it said that the excessive increase of audio-visual media in the rich countries is not always useful for the development of intelligence, particularly in children; on the contrary, it sometimes contributes to checking its development. The child lives only on sensations, he or she looks for ever-new sensations. . . . And thus the child becomes, without realizing it, a slave of this modern passion. Satiating oneself with sensations, one often remains passive intellectually; the intellect does not open to the search of truth; the will remains bound by habit, which it is unable to oppose.

It is seen from this that the modern person must fast, that is, abstain not only from food or drink, but from many other means of consumption, stimulation, satisfaction of the senses. To fast means to abstain, to renounce something. . . . This, in short, is the interpretation of fasting nowadays.

Renunciation of sensations, stimuli, pleasures, and even food or drink, is not an end in itself. It must only, so to speak, prepare the way for deeper contents by which the interior person "is nourished." This renunciation, this mortification, must serve to create in human beings the conditions to be able to live the superior values, for which all persons, in their own way, hunger. (80, pp. 1, 12)

For others, almsgiving. Today, we do not listen willingly to the word "alms." We feel something humiliating in it. This word seems to suppose a social system in which there reigns injustice, the unequal distribution of goods, a system that should be changed with adequate reforms. . . .

When the Lord Jesus speaks of alms, when he asks for almsdeeds to be practiced, he always does so in the sense of bringing help to those who need it, sharing one's own goods with the needy, that is, in the simple and essential sense, which does not permit us to doubt the value of the act denominated with the term "alms" but, on the contrary, urges us to approve it, as a good act, as an expression of love for one's neighbor, and as a salvific act.

Moreover, at a moment of particular importance, Christ utters these significant words: "The poor you always have with you" (Jn 12:8). He does not mean by these words that changes of social and economic structures are not important and that we should not try different ways to eliminate injustice, humiliation, want, and hunger. He means merely that human beings will have needs that cannot be satisfied unless with help for the needy and by sharing one's own goods with others. . . . Of what help are we speaking? What sharing? Is it only a question of alms, understood in the form of money, of material aid?

Certainly, Christ does not remove alms from our field of vision. He thinks also of pecuniary, material alms, but in his own way. More eloquent than any other, in this connection, is the example of the poor widow, who put a few small coins into the treasury of the temple: from the material point of view, an offering that could hardly be compared with the offerings given by others. Yet Christ said: "This poor widow has put in . . . all the living that she had" (Lk 21: 3–4). So it is, above all, the interior value of the gift that counts: the readiness to share everything, the readiness to give oneself. (82, pp. 1, 12)

For self, even play. Second, I know that you devote a great deal of time to play. Well, it is necessary to know that play is not just a matter of amusement and lightheartedness but, even when you do not realize it, is an important opportunity for formation and virtue. Also, in your future life, in fact, you will have to collaborate and also put yourselves against other persons, before problems, situations, and projects that, precisely, make life so similar to a game to be played fairly. To that, [you] will contribute the wise use of your own energies, clear knowledge of the general context in which you have taken your place, the capacity of adapting yourselves to the rhythm of others, and a loyal and generous sense of competition. That is why there can be no break between school and play; both contribute to building your personality, because both have a great deal to teach, and together they are the expression of a youth that is not only exterior but also interior. (142, p. 4)

It Is Necessary to Possess an Enlightened and Convinced Faith

All need a solid catechesis. You also are gathered here as disciples of Christ the Lord. Each one of you has become his disciple through holy baptism, which requires a solid preparation of our minds, our wills, and our hearts. This is done by means of catechesis, first of all in our families, then in the parish. By catechesis we search ever more deeply into the mystery of Christ, and we discover the meaning of our participation in it. Catechesis is not only learning religious concepts; it is an introduction to the life of participation in the mystery of Christ. (105, p. 90)

Furthermore, the baptized, if they wish to be Christians in works and in truth, must constantly remain faithful, during life, to the catechesis received. It tells them, in fact, how they must understand their Christianity and put it into practice in the various phases and environments of professional, social, and cultural life. This is the vast task of catechesis for adults. (96, p. 5)

You all need today a solid catechesis that may deepen your personal attachment to Jesus Christ and permit you to give account of the hope that is in you. I know that your pastoral activity devotes a great many efforts to this catechesis and to the formation of catechists. I congratulate you on that. Families, parishes, must give a priority to this formation, not only of children, but of young people, of students, of future spouses, in the framework too of preparation for the sacraments. Finally, I wish that your Christian communities may know the fervor of prayer and the strength of communal cohesion. . . . I wish, finally, that many lay Christians may also contribute their irreplaceable assistance to evangelization, as catechists, in an apostolate on a person-to-person basis, family to family, elder to younger. (152, p. 21)

Strengthened in experience. Today, particularly, it is necessary to possess an enlightened and convinced faith in order to be enlightening and convincing. The phenomenon of mass "culturization" calls for a deep, clear, and certain faith. For this reason, I exhort you to follow faithfully the teaching of the magisterium.

Only the one who has can give, and the Catholic Action militant is such precisely in order to give, to love, to enlighten, to save, to bring peace and joy. Catholic Action must aim resolutely at holiness.

Every commitment, even if it is of the social and charitable type, must never forget that what is essential in Christianity is the Redemption, that is, that Christ may be known, loved, and followed.

Commitment in holiness implies, therefore, austerity of life, serious control of one's tastes and choices, constant commitment in prayer, an attitude of obedience and docility to the directives of the Church, both in the doctrinal, moral, and pedagogical field, as well as in the liturgical one.

Today all people are in particular need of a smile, kindness, friendship. The great technical and social achievements, the spread of prosperity and of the permissive and consumer mentality, have not brought happiness. Divisions in the political field, the danger and the reality of new wars, continual calamities, implacable diseases, unemployment, the danger of ecological pollution, hatred and violence, and the many cases of despair have unfortunately created a stituation of continual tension and neurosis. (34, p. 8)

Exhorting you to commit yourselves with tireless dedication, I wish to encourage you in your effort to know our time, with its problems and its answers, with its questions, its conquests, and its defeats. Christians must realize the historical reality in which they live. Christians must be realistic and pick out fearlessly the characteristics of the society in which they are called to live.

Now, it is not difficult to see that in the philosophical and ideological field there is present a rationalistic, agnostic, and sometimes even antitheistic and anti-Christian mentality; for some people the only ideal is that of planned welfare and hedonism. The crisis of values has penetrated into the system of everyday life, into the structure of the family, into pedagogy, and into the very way of interpreting the meaning of existence and the significance of history.

Christians must realize this courageously, recalling, however, that not all values are destroyed, and there is a deep soul of truth, and that they must live in this historical context, trying to love everyone and to be a light on the lampstand and a leaven in the mass, in whatever situation they may find themselves. Enlightened and balanced knowledge of their own time makes Christians wisely optimistic and saves them from shutting themselves up in vain laments: every age of history must be understood and loved in order to be saved by Christ and by the Church. (182, p. 4)

And tested in daily work. Work is also the fundamental dimension of one's life on earth. Work has for each person a significance that is not merely technical but ethical. It can be said that human beings "subdue" the earth when by their behavior they become its masters, not its slaves, and also the masters and not the slaves of work.

Work must help people to become better, more mature spiritually, more responsible, in order that they may realize their vocation on earth both as unrepeatable persons and in community with others, especially in the fundamental human community constituted by the family. By joining together in this very community, whose character was established by the creator himself from the beginning, a man and a woman give life to new human beings. Work must make it possible for this human community to find the means necessary for its formation and maintenance. . . .

In every human work, prayer sets up a reference to God the creator and redeemer, and it also contributes to complete "humanization" of work. "Work exists . . . for resurrection" (C.K. Norwid). Human beings, indeed, are by their creator's will called from the beginning to subdue the earth by their work and also have been created in the image and after the likeness of God himself. There is no other way for them to find themselves and confirm who they are, except by seeking God in prayer. By seeking God, by seeking God, by meeting him. In prayer, human beings are bound to find themselves, since they are like God. They cannot find themselves except in his prototype. They cannot confirm their "dominion" over the earth by work except by praying at the same time. (104, p. 72)

Human beings can also love work for work's sake, because it enables them to take part in the great work of domination over the earth, a work that is planned by the creator. That love, it is true, corresponds to the dignity of the human being. (158, p. 56)

This ongoing formation is fostered in the Church community. In the community of the faithful—which must always maintain Catholic unity with the bishops and the Apostolic See—there are great insights of faith. The Holy Spirit is active in enlightening the minds of the faithful with his truth and in inflaming their hearts with his love. But these insights of faith and this *sensus fidelium* are not independent of the magisterium of the Church, which is an instrument of the same Holy Spirit and is assisted by him.

It is only when the faithful have been nourished by the word of God, faithfully transmitted in its purity and integrity, that their own charisms are fully operative and fruitful. Once the word of God is faithfully proclaimed to the community and is accepted, it brings forth fruits of justice and holiness of life in abundance.

But the dynamism of the community in understanding and living the word of God depends on its receiving intact the *depositum fidei,* and for this precise purpose a special apostolic and pastoral charism has been given to the Church. It is one and the same Spirit of truth who directs the hearts of the faithful and who guarantees the magisterium of the pastors of the flock. (125, p. 290)

And necessitates clear conscience formation. The connection between intelligence and will seems explicit above all in the act of conscience, that is, in the act in which each one evaluates the reason of good or evil inherent in a concrete action. To form one's own conscience appears, in this way, as a duty not to be postponed. To form one's conscience means discovering more and more clearly the light that starts one on the way to reaching in one's own conduct the true fullness of one's humanity. It is only by obeying the divine law that one realizes oneself fully as a person: "All have in their heart"—I am again quoting the Council—"a law written by God. To obey it is the very dignity of the person; according to it each one will be judged" (Constitution *Gaudium et Spes,* no. 16).

If the history of humanity, right from its first steps, is marked by the dramatic weakening produced by sin, it is also, however, and above all, the history of divine Love. The latter comes to us and, through the sacrifice of Christ our Redeemer, forgives our transgressions, illuminates consciences, and reintegrates the capacity of will to aim at good. Christ is the Way, the Truth, and the Life (cf. Jn 14:6); Christ guides all people, enlightens them, and vivifies them. Only with the grace of Christ, with his light and his strength, can human beings take their place at the supernatural level that belongs to them as children of God. Furthermore, only with this grace does it become possible for them to realize also all the good proportionate to their human nature itself.

Beloved in Christ, in your commitment for human dignity, for the defense of the interior unity of those who operate on different fronts of knowledge, the formation of consciences occupies, therefore, a preeminent place. (144, p. 5)

This enlightened faith is needed particularly by leaders. We must meet our human experience, our conscience. The first truth, proclaimed today, reminds human beings of their transience, recalls death, which is for each of us the end of earthly life. Today the Church lays great stress on this truth, confirmed by the history of every person. Remember that "to dust you shall return." Remember that your life on earth has a limit! (72, p. 5)

It is often the case that the great percentage of lay people who are zealously endeavoring as organized groups to permeate temporal affairs with the spirit of the gospel and to build genuine Christian communities come mostly from nonprofessional groups. Thus, an unfortunate impression is created that the leader/professional groups are not deeply interested in religious activities. In a country where the vast majority of people look up to the leaders and are easily encouraged by example, this apostolate of witness and example has great effectiveness and should be increasingly adopted. I sincerely hope that you can offer more and more of your talent and time in the service of the Church, in the lay apostolate of building up an authentic Christian community. Those, for example, who are recognized leaders in the field of health can do much to promote the Catholic principles regarding the intrinsic value of life in all its stages. Similarly, in the other professions, true Christian leadership is most effective.

May your efforts in this direction always be sustained by inflexible integrity of conduct, in the midst of the professional problems that you meet. But even more, may they be inspired by a desire to help those who are most in need, so that your service will be ruled by the criteria of justice and truth, of freedom and integrity, and be crowned with love. Remember always that as Christians you are called to live in accordance with the principles that you have learned from Christ and his Church. You are called to live upright lives consistent with your gospel principles.

Everyone is aware that the disciplines that you exercise call for constant renewal, in order that you may keep up with the rapid pace of new discoveries. Your capacity to adapt yourselves and to keep abreast of these developments will depend on your constant study of the basic principles underlying these disciplines. And may your Catholic faith also be constantly renewed; may it grow deeper and develop, through the radical dynamism of constant conversion to Christ, a conversion animated by a life lived according to the gospel and in harmony with the magisterium, nourished by a life of personal piety based upon prayer and the reception of the sacraments. May the testimony of your faith shine brightly in your professional lives, as well as in your personal and family lives. (215, p. 10)

This (Constitution *Gaudium et Spes,*, nos. 27, 51) is the context in which your commitment is set. It consists in the first place of an intelligent and assiduous action to make consciences become aware of the inviolability of human life at all its stages, so that the right to it will be effectively recognized in morals and in laws, as a basic value of every society that wants to call itself civil. It is expressed in a courageous stand against every form of attack on life, from whatever quarter it may come. Finally, it takes the form of a disinterested and respected offer of concrete help for persons who are up against difficulties in making their behavior conform with the dictates of conscience. . . .

Do not be discouraged by the difficulties, opposition, and failure you may meet with on your way. It is a question of humanity, and with such a stake, you cannot shut yourselves up in an attitude of resigned passivity without thereby abdicating as human beings. (70, p. 8)

CHAPTER 5

MINISTRY OF LAITY

One and the same Spirit has summoned your service in the Church into life.

Each one of us is handpicked. All are called to ministry to prolong and extend the work of Christ. This ministry is extensive and can be greatly aided by joint effort in Christian groups.

You are called to exercise a particular ecclesial role.

John Paul II rejoices in the increased participation of laity in the Church's life and ministry. Laity are now involved in the ministry of catechesis, Catholic schools and education, and evangelization through the media. Also important are community building, service to the sick, and Christian witness to the world. The Pope urges laity to hold fast when problems develop in the ministry.

Laity are called to be involved in the world in order to transform it according to the gospel.

Laity contribute to the evangelization of the world by the quality of their Christian lives, by their dedication as good citizens, by their presence, which reveals the true meaning of life. They are called to the ministries of charity and social justice.

I call upon you to sanctify work.

The value of work is enhanced by Jesus. Laity must challenge its unjust aspects, develop a spirituality of work, and offer the world a new perspective on life and work.

One and the Same Spirit Has Summoned Your Service in the Church Into Life

Each one of us is handpicked. It is essential for us to understand that Jesus has a specific task in life for each and every one of us. Each one of us is handpicked, called by name—by Jesus! There is no one among us who does not have a divine vocation! Now this is what St. Paul wrote in his letter to the Ephesians, which was proclaimed a few moments ago: "Each one of us has been given our own share of grace, given as Christ allotted it. And to some, his gift was that they should be apostles; to some, prophets; to some, evangelists; to some, pastors and teachers; so that the saints make a unity in the work of service" (Eph 4:7, 11–12).

First and foremost, God has called us into existence. He has called us to be! He has called us, through his Son Jesus Christ, to a knowledge of himself as our loving Father. He has called us to be his children! He has called us to fulfill his eternal plan in our individual lives, with Jesus as our guide. He has called us to be co-heirs with Jesus of his heavenly Kingdom! What God our Father is offering us through his Son is a new life as his real children, with Jesus for our brother; a pressing call to live, to love, to labor for the coming of his Kingdom. And lest, bewildered at what we must do, we hesitate, Jesus offers to be himself our guide and says, "Come, follow me!" (Lk 9:59). (272, p. 16)

You have been called by God to the life of community, of Church. And once again, it is a matter of a grace: it was the Lord who brought you together in Church, who made you Church, united to the whole ecclesial Body spread throughout the entire world.

God's gift that has been given you is the sign that you are loved by him. So, to be a Christian is not, first of all, to take on an endless number of commitments and obligations, but to let oneself be loved by God, just as Christ himself, who is and feels loved by the Father, consistently testified with his whole life and says explicitly: "The Father loves me" (Jn 10:17).

Our profession of faith begins with these words: "I believe in God the Father." In these words the entire Christian attitude is summed up: to let oneself be loved by God as a father. Each of us is loved by God and is known by name as a child. This is why it is always possible to turn to him with faith. It was Christ, as an "older brother," who taught us this.

Loved by God, therefore, you will certainly ask, "What must we as lay persons do?" Christians can never limit themselves to a purely passive attitude, only to receive. To each of us is given a different gift, according to the outpouring of the Spirit, but for the common good.

From this, from the very nature of being baptized, stems the need for the apostolate in the Church, which is a sacrament established by Christ to reach all people, and for this reason it is continuously given new life by the Holy Spirit.

Your mission as lay persons, therefore, is basically the sanctification of the world, through your personal sanctification, for the restoration of the world. The Second Vatican Council, which was so concerned with the laity and their role in the Church, very well emphasized their secular nature. It is the Christian who lives in the world who is responsible for the Christian building up of the temporal order in its various sectors: in the political and cultural areas, in the arts, in industry, in commerce, in agriculture. . . .

The Church must be present in all areas of human activity, and nothing that is human can remain extraneous to it. And it is principally you, dear lay people, who must make it present. When the Church is accused of being absent from some area or of not being concerned about some human problem, it would be equivalent to being upset by the absence of wise lay people or of the inactivity of Christians in that specific area of human life. For this reason I address a warm appeal to you: do not let the Church be absent in any environment of the life of your dear nation. Everything must be permeated by the leaven of the gospel of Christ and illuminated by its light. It is your duty to do it! (266, p. 14)

All are called to ministry. There exists, therefore, a great space for our solidarity with Christ, a great space for the apostolate of all, for the apostolate of the laity in particular. Unfortunately, it becomes impossible once more in the framework of this short homily to make a more detailed analysis of this subject. However, the words of today's liturgy urge us to reread them again, to meditate on them and to put into practice all that has become, in such ample dimensions, the subject of the teaching of the Council on the lay apostolate. In the past the concept of the apostolate seemed to be almost reserved only for those who are "in their official capacity" the successors of the Apostles, who express and guarantee the apostolicity of the Church. The Second Vatican Council revealed what large fields of apostolate were always accessible to the laity. At the same time it again stimulated to this apostolate. It is enough to quote just one sentence of the decree *Apostolicam Actuositatem,* which in a certain sense contains and sums up everything: "The Christian vocation is of its nature a vocation to the apostolate as well" (n. 2). (20, p. 10)

The Second Vatican Council deepened the idea of priesthood and presented it throughout its teaching as the expression of the inner "dynamisms" whereby the mission of the whole people of God in the Church is constituted. Here one should refer especially to the constitution *Lumen Gentium* and reread carefully the relevant paragraphs. The mission of the people of God is carried out through the sharing in the office and mission of Jesus Christ himself, which, as we know, has a triple dimension: It is the mission and office of prophet, priest, and king. If we analyze carefully the conciliar texts, it is obvious that one should speak of a triple dimension of Christ's service and mission rather than of three different functions. . . . As Christians, members of the people of God, and subsequently as priests, sharers in the hierarchical order, we take our origin from the combination of the mission and office of our teacher, who is prophet, priest, and king, in order to witness to him in a special way in the Church and before the world. . . .

We must consider down to the smallest detail not only the theoretical meaning of the mutual relation that exists between the hierarchical priesthood and the common priesthood of the faithful. The fact that they differ not only in degree but also in essence is a fruit of a particular aspect of the richness of the very priesthood of Christ, which is the one center and the one source both of that participation that belongs to all the baptized and of that other participation that is reached through a distinct sacrament. (92, pp. 697–698)

To prolong and extend the work of Christ. Jesus needs you because his love will not reach the world without the witness of your Christian lives. Jesus cannot be fully present in your cities and villages, in your families and schools, in your workshops or in the fields where you toil, unless you, the lay people, bring him there, manifest him there by what you say and do, make him visible in your love for each other. (219, p. 617)

Fidelity to one's vocation, that is to say, persevering readiness for "kingly service," has particular significance for these many forms of building, especially with regard to the most exigent tasks, which have more influence on the life of our neighbor and of the whole of society. Married people must be distinguished for fidelity to their vocation, as is demanded by the indissoluble nature of the sacramental institution of marriage. . . . They must endeavor with all their strength to persevere in their matrimonial union, building up the family community through this witness of love and educating new generations of men and women, capable in their turn of dedicating the whole of their lives to their vocation, that is to say, to the "kingly service" of which Jesus Christ has offered us the example and the most beautiful model. (73, p. 642)

Having been called by Christ himself, you are his chosen partners in evangelization. This leads you to share the Church's zeal to provide Catholic religious education for all Catholic children in all types of educational institutions. You are truly aware of the mystery of the Church, that all of us who are baptized in Christ make up his Body, the Church. In this Church there is diversity of apostolate or ministry but oneness of mission: the spreading of the Kingdom of Christ. Bishops, priests, religious, and laity—each group has its specific contribution to make. (260, p. 6)

The lay ministry is extensive. As lay people, you know that your special apostolate is to bring Christian principles to bear upon the temporal order, that is, to bring the spirit of Christ into such spheres of life as marriage and the family, trade and commerce, the arts and professions, politics and government, culture and national and international relations. In all these areas lay people must, in the expression of the Second Vatican Council, play their own distinctive role (cf. Constitution *Gaudium et Spes*, no. 43). . . .

In society you are called to be a leaven for Christ: to witness to Christ in the school, in the government office, in the company works, in the club gathering, in the town development union, in age grade meetings, in the market, in the trade union, and in politics. In all these secular spheres you will promote justice, unity, honesty, and public-spiritedness. Together you will seek gospel-inspired and concrete answers to problems of bribery, corruption, lack of discipline, ethnicism, and other such evils.

In your Church organizations you will be models of unity, discipline, hard work, loyalty to your leaders, forgetfulness of self, rejoicing when others have done well, not seeking fame but only the Kingdom of Christ, and not struggling for the first place in society or wanting to be called master: "For you have one master, the Christ" (Mt 23:10).

It is above all in the family that you will be able to communicate Christ. You will be exemplary husbands and wives, setting up a community of love and life, and exercising as fathers and mothers a real ministry in educating your children. It is through you that members are provided for the Body of Christ, and candidates for the priesthood and religious life. Nigeria looks to you with confidence to train good citizens for society.

As you engage in your numerous initiatives in the apostolate, you will place great importance on prayer and union with Christ. I am happy to know that your chaplains emphasize this, that you receive the Sacrament of Reconciliation often, that the Holy Eucharist is the center of your Christian lives and of all your activities. Indeed, your evangelizing zeal comes above all from the Eucharist. With God's grace, the days of recollection and the yearly retreats that you hold for spiritual rejuvenation can also help you to continue to grow in the faith that you have received. (260, p. 6)

And can be greatly aided by joint effort in Christian groups. The individual lay apostolate, made up of personal activities and, above all, of Christian witness, must be united with the associate forms of the apostolate in which the laity join to achieve certain objectives together. Instead of excluding each other, the two forms complete each other. No associate form of the apostolate is effective without the personal witness of every member. On the other hand, in view of modern needs, which greatly surpass individual capacities, a united effort is needed to carry the gospel message to the heart of civilization.

Many movements and types of organizations of the lay apostolate exist; all are important and useful if imbued with a truly ecclesial and Christian spirit of service. Each one has its objectives, with methods suitable to its area and to its surroundings; but it is indispensable to be aware of this complementary nature and to establish bonds of esteem between them so that their dialogue will establish a certain union of effort and also true cooperation. We belong to the same Church. We must encourage each other to do good. We must all work together for the same cause. Christ is only one. Although the ministries and activities are many, all lead to the same end: that Christ be proclaimed, that humanity be saved, that the common good be served, and finally, that God be glorified in every thing. (266, p. 14)

You Are Called to Exercise a Particular Ecclesial Role

John Paul II rejoices in the increased participation of laity in the Church's life and ministry. I am anxious to give thanks in the Church's name to all of you, lay teachers of catechesis in the parishes, the men and the still more numerous women throughout the world, who are devoting yourselves to the religious education of many generations. Your work is often lowly and hidden, but it is carried out with ardent and generous zeal, and it is an eminent form of the lay apostolate, a form that is particularly important where for various reasons children and young people do not receive suitable religious training in the home.

How many of us have received from people like you our first notions of catechism and our preparation for the sacrament of penance, for our first communion and confirmation! The fourth general assembly of the synod did not forget you. I join with it in encouraging you to continue your collaboration for the life of the Church. (129, p. 346)

I rejoice also at all that has been done in this country to endow the Church with lay catechists and leaders of small communities, who are the durable workers of evangelization, in constant and direct contact with families, children, the various categories of the people of God. All this deployment of the indispensable activity of the laity in close communion with its pastors must certainly be favored. (149, p. 7)

I encourage you . . . to exercise your individual and corporate responsibility for increasing catechetical instruction as you endeavor to implement fully the social teachings of the Church. Be fully convinced of how important it is for every future generation . . . to be aware of the supreme dignity to which they are called, which is eternal life in Christ Jesus. (216, p. 616)

Laity are now involved in the ministry of catechesis. Catechesis certainly constitutes a permanent and also fundamental form of activity by the Church, one in which her prophetic charism is manifested: witnessing and teaching go hand in hand. And although here we are speaking in the first place of priests, it is, however, impossible not to mention also the great number of men and women religious dedicating themselves to catechetical activity for love of the divine master. Finally, it would be difficult not to mention the many lay people who find expression in this activity for their faith and their apostolic responsibility.

Furthermore, increasing care must be taken that the various forms of catechesis and its various fields—beginning with the fundamental field, family catechesis, that is, the catechesis by parents of their children—should give evidence of the universal sharing by the whole of the people of God in the prophetic office of Christ himself. (73, p. 639)

The Church recognizes in these catechists people called to exercise a particular ecclesial role, a special sharing in the responsibility for the advancement of the gospel. She sees them as witnesses of faith, servants of Jesus Christ and his Church, effective collaborators in the mission of establishing, developing, and fostering the life of the Christian community. In the history of evangelization many of these catechists have in fact been teachers of religion, leaders in their communities, zealous lay missionaries, and examples of faith. They have stood faithfully by the missionaries and the local clergy, supporting their ministry while fulfilling their own distinctive task. The catechists have rendered many services connected with communicating Christ, implanting the Church and bringing the transforming and regenerative power of the gospel ever more into the lives of their brothers and sisters. They have assisted people in many human needs and contributed to development and progress. (156, p. 9)

What do you need, my dear catechists, in order to elicit the proper response to Christ's message of life? You need to be faithful to Christ, to his Church, and to humanity.

You must be faithful first of all to Christ, to his truth, to his mandate; otherwise there would be distortion, betrayal. As catechists you are, after all, echoes of Christ (cf. Apostolic Exhortation *Catechesi Tradendae*, no. 6). The Church too should be the object of your consistent faithfulness. For catechesis, which is growth in faith and the maturing of the Christian life, is a work that Christ wills to accomplish in his Church. An authentic catechist must necessarily be an ecclesial catechist. Finally, you must be faithful to humanity, for the Lord's Word and message is intended for every human being. Not an abstract, imaginary person, but the individual who lives in time, with his or her difficulties, problems, and hopes. It is to this person that the gospel must be proclaimed, so that through it he or she may receive from the Holy Spirit the light and strength to come to full Christian maturity. To a large extent, the effectiveness of catechesis will depend on its capacity to give meaning, Christian meaning, to everything that constitutes human life in this world. (215, p. 11)

Catholic schools and education. The Church's responsibility for divine truth must be increasingly shared in various ways by all. What shall we say at this point with regard to the specialists in the various levels and with different specializations? As members of the people of God, they all have their own part to play in Christ's prophetic mission and service of divine truth, among other ways, by an honest attitude toward truth, whatever field it may belong to, while educating others in truth and teaching them to mature in love and justice. Thus, a sense of responsibility for truth is one of the fundamental points of encounter between the Church and each person and also one of the fundamental demands determining each person's vocation in the community of the Church. (73, p. 639)

You teach religion in the Church's behalf in schools and similar institutions as your specialty. . . . First, you need a high degree of competence in this regard. You need qualified training and good theology. Faith draws understanding of the faith from its inner dynamic: *fides quaerens intellectum* (faith seeking understanding). From one point of view it is like some substance that demands entire and tireless efforts of research and keeps it going. (192, p. 393)

The teaching of scholastic subjects and the use of the teaching aids necessary for instruction take their place in the wider program of that Christian *paideia,* which in turn takes its place in the evangelizing mission entrusted to the Church by her divine Founder. (33, p. 12)

It is clear how important are the studies of those who, in their concern for a deeper knowledge of it, investigate the mystery of Christ. Appreciate your task! Appreciate the importance of your presence in the Church! (131, p. 394)

Young people, I say to you, Christ is waiting for you with open arms; Christ is relying on you to build justice and peace, to spread love. As in Turin, I say again today: You must return to the school of Christ . . . to rediscover the true, full, deep meaning of these words. The necessary support for these values lies only in possession of a sure and sincere faith, a faith that embraces God and humanity, humanity in God. . . . There is not a more adequate, a deeper dimension to give to this word "humanity," to this word "love," to this word "freedom," to the words "peace" and "justice": there is nothing else, there is only Christ. (202, p. 496)

I wish for all of you that healthy optimism . . . optimism that takes its mysterious but real origin from the God in whom you have your faith, or from the unknown God toward whom tends the truth that is the object of your enlightened investigations.

May the science of which you make profession, academicians and scientists, in the domain of pure research as in that of applied research, help humanity, with the support of religion and in agreement with it, to find again the path of hope and to attain the final goal of peace and faith! (134, p. 392)

As regards Catholic schools, I joyfully approve of the initiative that sets out to ensure the special Christian formation of the laity who serve in the ranks of educators in our schools. The educational apostolate is congenial to them. The truly ecclesial testimony of lay people must have a particular importance among pupils, who being mostly called to married life will be able to see in their teachers a model to be imitated unreservedly. It is to be hoped that the presence of excellent fathers and mothers of families among the teachers of Catholic schools will remove the cause for the complaints that are sometimes heard among parents, concerned because of certain questionable forms of expression on delicate subjects such as religion or sex education. (226, p. 12)

And evangelization through the media. We are very conscious of the part radio and television play in the life of the world and in the life of the Church, and of the capacity of the media to unite people in the celebration of events that deeply touch their lives. . . . (5, p. 9)

The motivation that principally impels your work is the evangelization of the human race, which requires a clear and explicit proclamation of salvation in Jesus Christ, a proclamation of his teaching, his life, his promises, his kingdom, and his mystery as the Son of the living God and the Son of Mary (cf. Apostolic Exhortation *Evangelii Nuntiandi,* nos. 22, 27). (5, p. 9)

This evangelization must be done through a thoroughly competent and professional use of radio, television, and the audiovisual media. And with evangelization are necessarily linked the advancement of the whole human race and the integral development of all men and women in the world. This is a noble and deeply Christian aim, and the Pope is with you in your conviction that it can be served worthily only by a professionalism that admits of nothing carelessly prepared. . . .

Have no doubt that your labors and efforts are necessary in our world today. The Church needs you, appreciates you, and confidently depends on you, in your specialized area of service to the Catholic faith. (5, p. 10)

To speak of the cinema is, in the first place, to call to mind the very complex sector of creativity and of film production. A real dialogue must be established here between the Church and the world of the cinema; you are already, and you can increasingly be, its qualified and effective architects. May you contribute to the bringing forth of a new mentality that accepts that priorities be clearly established! Here are some subjects on which you could meditate deeply with producers and actors: Do they seek the promotion of real human value? Do they give religious and specifically Christian values their rightful place? You can at least insist that the latter should not be omitted or underestimated. What a responsibility for the Church and also what a hope, continually to encourage a return to a film production that is humanly worthy of the name! (9, p. 4)

It is my wish precisely that craftsmen of religious information may always find the help they need from competent ecclesial organisms. The latter must receive them in respect—for their convictions and their profession supply them with very adequate and objective documentation—but also propose to them a Christian perspective that sets facts in their true significance for the Church and for humanity. In this way you will be able to tackle these religious reports with the specific competence that they demand.

You are very concerned about freedom of information and of expression: you are right. Think yourselves lucky to enjoy it! Use this freedom well to grasp the truth more closely and to admit your readers, your listeners, or your viewers into "whatever is true, whatever is honorable, whatever is just, whatever is pure, whatever is lovely, whatever is gracious," to repeat the words of St. Paul (Phil 4:8), into what helps them to live in justice and community, to discover the ultimate meaning of life, to open them up to the mystery of God, so near each of us. Under these conditions, your profession, so demanding and sometimes so exhausting—I was going to say your vocation—so topical and so beautiful, will elevate further the spirit and the heart of all people of good will, at the same time as the faith of Christians. It is a service that the Church and humanity appreciate. (3, p. 4)

Also important are community building. The community of the people of God that constitutes the Church in your country has brought, in the course of its long history through the centuries and especially in recent generations, a wealth of useful gifts to the unity of the universal Church and to all its individual parts. I willingly give homage here to the exceptional contribution that the Netherlands made to the missionary activity of the universal Church. The Catholic church in the Netherlands can also rejoice because of what it has accomplished in the domain of education, in the care of the sick and those on the margins of society, and in the apostolate of the laity. This synod will examine afresh the life of the Church in the Netherlands with regard to the tasks that condition its witness in the face of present society and vis-a-vis the contribution that it is always called to give to the Church's universal mission. (139, p. 524)

Service to the sick. Now at the beginning of our universal pastoral ministry, we wish to open to [the weak, the poor, the sick, and those afflicted with sorrow] our heart. Do not you, brothers and sisters, share by your sufferings in the passion of our Redeemer, and in a certain way complete it? (cf. Col 1:24). The unworthy successor of St. Peter who proposes to explore the "unsearchable riches of Christ" (Eph 3:8) has the greatest need of your help, your prayers, your devotedness, or "sacrifice," and this he most humbly asks of you. (1, p. 4)

All this can be summed up in one word, which only apparently may seem usual and common: it is the word "service," to be understood as a struggle against disease and a commitment to the sick. Yours is actually a service of life, or even better, of the living human beings, that is, human beings who—as a great Father of the ancient Church says—precisely because they are living, are, in the concrete, the glory of God (St. Irenaeus, *Adversus Haereses* 4.20.7).

From the depth of this perspective there emerges all the grandeur and nobility of the medical profession, which is at the same time an art and a science, because alongside a serious doctrinal preparation it requires keen psychological intuition. If life is a gift from God . . . it must constitute for you the terminal and inescapable reference point, to which you must continually look in all the individual services and phases in which the exercise of such a delicate art is carried out. Your service is addressed precisely to the living person, from the first moment in which this ever new and amazing mystery of life buds, thus deriving immediately the character of sacredness. Here is the first principle, the absolute principle, which concerns professional ethics and does not admit of exceptions and violations: it must be, therefore—and I hope it will always be—a part of honor. (201, p. 14)

Never be satisfied with what you have done and never let the difficulties tire you. Read in the eyes and in the hearts of those who bear the cross of their mutilations and disability, having to sustain hard struggles, often hidden from others, but known to God and strengthened by faith in him. Be close to those you assist and let them feel the warmth of your true friendship, which like a fragrant balm can comfort so many sufferings. (224, p. 10)

Millions of sightless sisters and brothers are waiting, if not for the miracle of a cure, for understanding, solidarity, affection, and help from us; in a word, for our true charity, based on faith. And it is this very faith that must operate in us by means of charity (cf. Gal 5:6), as St. Paul tells us. Keep well in mind the recommendation of Jesus: "Let your light so shine before all, that they may see your good works and give glory to your Father who is in heaven" (Mt 5:16). Continue this apostolic work of yours with enthusiasm, with commitment. Do not let yourselves be cast down by difficulties or discouragement. (24, p. 4)

And Christian witness to the world. This is, therefore, the testimony that the Christian community and even the world of culture expect from you, teachers and pupils of the university . . . to prove with facts that intelligence is not only not impaired, but on the contrary stimulated and strengthened by that incomparable source of understanding human reality, which is the Word of God; to show with facts that it is possible to build around this Word a community of men and women . . . to carry on their research in the different areas without losing contact with the essential frame of reference of a Christian view of life; a community of men and women who seek particular answers to particular problems but who are sustained by the joyful awareness of possessing together the ultimate answer to ultimate problems; a community of men and women, above all, who endeavor to incarnate, in their existence and in the social environment to which they belong, the proclamation of salvation that they received from him who is "the true light that enlightens everyone" (Jn 1:9). (22, p. 10)

This is once more a testimony of the Christian world by which the whole of our culture is penetrated. And since the language of music is more universal than that of literature, I hope that this fruit of the artistic creativity of a fellow countryman of mine may become cause of artistic emotions in all contemporaries, regardless of their nationality. (61, p. 8)

Hence, as young Catholic university students you have a special testimony to give. Not to give it would be to deprive humanity of an expert and necessary contribution, one that can be made only by someone who is proud to be in the ranks of Christ's followers.

Dear young people, the mission that Christ gives you is a universal one, but at the same time it is to be realized in a unique way by each one of you. The particular way the mission is carried out depends on the missionaries, on you. It is up to you to discover all the right ways of fulfilling the Lord's mission in your world of young university students. (217, p. 596)

The Pope urges laity to hold fast when problems develop in the ministry. No one has any illusions about this: service to our neighbor can turn into pure routine. How poor is he who treats it as a mere livelihood with relative payment and settled working times, without love of neighbor and the gospel being able to draw him to undertake labor out of the fixed time. Yet tedium comes to those, too, who would consume themselves in this service for the sake of the good, who would serve the Church because acceptance of Jesus' message is linked with the Church's credibility. Compassion passes, generosity is used up, the heart becomes disappointed. (192, p. 392)

Many are of the opinion that readiness to give human lives the support of the faith cannot be turned into a profession. This is absolutely out of touch with the times. And since the future shape of this service is not yet quite clear and is often incalculable, the choice made seems in the eyes of many to be senseless.

Hold fast to this, even if further clarification of your calling's form will still require reflection. If you do not receive from everyone in the communities that acceptance and welcome that you have so far experienced and that you have hoped for, it seems important to me that you should go on intelligently, in hard situations above all, and remind yourselves of the idealism of your beginnings and try to win over other collaborators and communities gradually. We all believe that one and the same Spirit, who guides the communities and hearts of all people, has summoned your service in the Church into life. You are called to entrust yourselves to this Spirit precisely when faced with trouble. (192, p. 394)

Laity Are Called to Be Involved in the World in Order to Transform It According to the Gospel

Laity contribute to the evangelization of the world. As the bishop proclaims the dignity of the laity, it is also his role to do everything possible to promote their contribution to evangelization, urging them to assume every responsibility that is theirs in temporal realities. In the words of Paul VI: "Their own field of evangelizing activity is the vast and complicated world of politics, society and economics, the world of culture, of the sciences and the arts, of international life, of mass media" (Apostolic Exhortation *Evangelii Nuntiandi,* no. 70). And there are other spheres of activities in which they can effectively work for the transformation of society.

In accordance with the will of God, the Christian family is an evangelizing agent of immense importance. . . . (117, p. 322)

To God's call, however, there must correspond an adequate answer on our part. What answer? The one that has its basic outline in baptism and that becomes conscious and responsible in the act of personal faith, brought forth by listening to the Word, nourished by participation in the sacraments, witnessed by a life in Christ inspired by the beatitudes, and that strives generously to carry out his commandments, the greatest of which is the commandment of love.

Within this common vocation, which God addresses to every human being, there stand out the specific vocations, by means of which God "chooses" individual persons for a particular task. These are, as is obvious, multiple and complementary vocations, identical as regards purpose, communion with God, but different as regards the ways and means necessary to attain it.

I am thinking, for example, from the point of view of one's profession, of the choice of a certain type of study and specialization, in the perspective of a given type of work, from which one certainly expects earnings for oneself but also the possibility of making a personal contribution to the construction of a better world. I am thinking above all, from the point of view of state of life, of the choice of marriage, of that of giving birth to a new human being or of adopting a child that has been left alone in the world, etc. And I am thinking also of other situations: for example, of the husband who is left a widower, of the spouse who is abandoned, of the orphan. I am thinking of the condition of the sick; of the old, infirm and lonely; and of the poor: "God chose what is weak in the world," St. Paul recalled, "to shame the strong." In God's mysterious plan, the renewing action of grace passes through human weakness: it passes particularly, therefore, through these situations of suffering and abandonment. (211, p. 6)

The Church wishes to serve people also in the temporal dimension of their life and existence. Given the fact that this dimension is realized through people's membership in the various communities—national and state, and therefore at the same time social, political, economic, and cultural—the Church continually rediscovers her own mission in relationship to these sectors of human life and activity. . . .

By establishing a religious relationship with people, the Church consolidates them in their natural social bonds. . . . The Church . . . has always sought . . . to train sons and daughters who are of assistance to the state, good citizens and useful and creative workers in the various spheres of social, professional, and cultural life. And this derives from the fundamental mission of the Church, which everywhere and always strives to make people better, more conscious of their dignity, and more devoted in their lives to their family, social, professional, and patriotic commitments. It is her mission to make people more confident, more courageous, conscious of their rights and duties, socially responsible, creative, and useful. (101, p. 53)

By the quality of their Christian lives. Only when Christians faithfully preserve their own identity will they be able to make their specific contribution to the building of a society that is really in conformity with the whole measure of the human being's truth and dignity. In this way Christians, on the strength of this identity of theirs, will be able to confront all the more effectively all those who are engaged in contributing to the building up of the same society and to humanity's real progress. Otherwise they become that salt that has lost its taste, of which the Gospel speaks, no longer good for anything except to be thrown out and trampled under foot by others (cf. Mt 5:13 and Dogmatic Constitution *Lumen Gentium*, no. 33). (242, p. 8)

The lifestyle of many members of our rich and permissive societies is easy, and so is the lifestyle of increasing groups inside the poorer countries. As I said last year to the plenary assembly of the Pontifical Commission on Justice and Peace, "Christians will want to be in the vanguard in favoring ways of life that decisively break with the frenzy of consumerism, exhausting and joyless" (Nov. 11, 1978). It is not a question of slowing down progress, for there is no human progress when everything conspires to give full reign to the instincts of self-interest, sex, and power. We must find a simple way of living. For it is not right that the standard of living of the rich countries should seek to maintain itself by draining off a great part of the reserves of energy and raw materials that are meant to serve the whole of humanity. For readiness to create a greater and more equitable solidarity between peoples is the first condition of peace. . . .

It is in joyful simplicity of a life inspired by the gospel and the gospel's spirit of communal sharing that you will find the best remedy for sour criticism, paralyzing doubt, and the temptation to make money the principal means and indeed the very measure of advancement. (121, p. 311)

Be faithful to Christ and joyfully embrace his gospel of salvation. Do not be tempted by ideologies that preach only material values or purely temporal ideals, which separate political, social, and economic development from the things of the spirit and in which happiness is sought apart from Christ. The road toward your total liberation is not the way of violence, class struggle, or hate; it is the way of love, community, and peaceful solidarity. I know that you understand me . . . for you are blessed and possess the kingdom of heaven. (216, p. 616)

By their dedication as good citizens. The Church, an expert on humanity, faithful to the signs of the times and expert on obedience to the urgent invitation of the last council, today wants to continue its mission of faith and defense of human rights. She invites Christians to commit themselves to constructing a more just, humane, and habitable world that does not close itself in but rather opens itself to God.

Making this world more just means, among other things, to make the effort, to strive to have a world in which no more children lack sufficient nutrition, education, instruction; that there be no more children without proper formation; that there be no more poor peasants without land, so that they can live and develop with dignity; that there be no more workers mistreated nor whose rights are lessened; that there be no more systems that permit the exploitation of one person by another person or by the state; that there be no more corruption; that there be no more who have too much while others are lacking everything through no fault of their own; that there not be so many families who are broken, disunited, insufficiently attended; that there be no injustice or inequality in administering justice; that there be no one who is not supported by the law and that the law support everyone equally; that force not prevail over truth and rights, but rather truth and rights over force; and that the economic and political never prevail over the human.

But do not be content with a more human world. Make an explicitly more divine world, more according to God, governed by faith and that which faith inspires—the moral, religious, and social progress of humanity. Do not lose sight of the vertical orientation of evangelization. It can liberate humanity, because it is the revelation of love. The love of the Father for human beings, for all and each person, love revealed by Jesus Christ. (47, p. 543)

Christians, therefore, and especially you who are laity, are called by God to be involved in the world in order to transform it according to the gospel.

In carrying out this task, your own personal commitment to truth and honesty plays an important role, because a sense of responsibility for the truth is one of the fundamental points of encounter between the Church and each man and woman (cf. Encyclical *Redemptor Hominis,* no. 19).

The Christian faith does not provide you with ready-made solutions to the complex problems affecting contemporary society. But it does give you deep insights into the nature of human beings and their needs, calling you to speak the truth in love, to take up your responsibilities as good citizens, and to work with your neighbors to build a society where true human values are nourished and deepened by a shared Christian vision of life. (154, p. 27)

The duties of the good Christian citizen involve more than shunning corruption, more than not exploiting others. These duties include positively contributing to the establishment of just laws and structures that foster human values. If the Christian finds injustice or anything that militates against love, peace, and unity in society, he or she must ask: "Where have I fallen short? What have I done wrong? What did I fail to do that the truth of my vocation called me to do? Did I sin by omission?" (154, p. 27)

By their presence, which reveals the true meaning of life. To evangelize means making Christ present in the life of the person and, at the same time, in the life of society. To evangelize means doing everything possible, according to our capacities, in order that all "may believe," in order that all may find themselves again in Christ, in order that they may find again in him the meaning and the adequate dimension of their own life. This finding again is, at the same time, the deepest source of human liberation. St. Paul expresses this when he writes, "It was for liberty that Christ freed us" (Gal 5:1). So liberation, then, is certainly a reality of faith, one of the fundamental biblical themes that are a deep part of Christ's salvific mission, of the work of redemption, of his teaching. This subject has never ceased to constitute the content of the spiritual life of Christians. (68, p. 600)

Christians have the right and the duty to contribute so far as they are able to building up society. And they do so through association and institutional frameworks that a free society operates with participation by all. . . .

So all communities of Christians, both basic communities and parishes, diocesan communities, or the whole national church community ought to make their specific contributions to building up society. All human concerns must be taken into consideration. (166, p. 139)

Do I then make a mistake when I tell you, Catholic youth, that it is part of your task in the world and the Church to reveal the true meaning of life where hatred, neglect, or selfishness threaten to take over the world? . . . I propose to you the option of love, which is the opposite of escape. If you really accept that love from Christ, it will lead you to God. Perhaps in the priesthood or religious life; perhaps in some special service to your brothers and sisters, especially to the needy, the poor, the lonely, the abandoned, those whose rights have been trampled upon, or those whose basic needs have not been provided for. Whatever you make of your life, let it be something that reflects the love of Christ. The whole people of God will be all the richer because of the diversity of your commitments. In whatever you do, remember that Christ is calling you, in one way or another, to the service of love: the love of God and of your neighbor. . . .

Dear young people, do not be afraid of honest effort and honest work; do not be afraid of the truth. With Christ's help, and through prayer, you can answer his call, resisting temptations and fads and every form of mass manipulation. Open your hearts to the Christ of the gospels—to his love and his truth and his joy. (120, p. 268)

This evangelization of the personal and collective conscience of humanity must therefore be pursued according to ways that are similar in the whole Church, but whose concrete application you must find here, in keeping with your African culture and your present situation. There is in the first place the witness of your Christian life, that of families, of adults and young people, of consecrated persons: your Christian way of living can stimulate, by itself and in full respect for others, the attraction of the gospel. (152, p. 21)

They are called to the ministries of charity. You want to serve your country. You are concerned about the poor. And you know that a soulless civilization would not bring happiness. You are ready to devote to this work your labor and your honesty, in respect for all, while banishing hatred, violence, and lying. Those who have responsibility for the common good cannot be unaware that your Christian contribution is beneficial to the country. (152, p. 22)

Even if public welfare services are gradually covering tasks carried out for centuries by the charity of the Church, and even if modern society is trying to meet certain social security and welfare requirements in an institutional and organic form, the welfare and charitable action of the Church has not at all lost its irreplaceable function in the modern world.

Charity will always be necessary, as a stimulus and completion of justice itself; it will always remain for the Church the sign of its testimony and its credibility (cf. Jn 13:35).

Be inwardly convinced of the necessity of your work, of the right and the duty you have to carry it out: a work that you will want to promote tirelessly, defending its meaning and urgency and its free exercise; improving its methods and services; committing yourselves also for a harmonious and unified effort so that the various welfare institutions, without losing their own nature and autonomy, will be able to act in a spirit of sincere collaboration with one another and thus facilitate opportune and useful interventions of the public authorities and an adequate legislation. (90, p. 11)

And social justice. It is obvious, in fact, that in the name of alleged justice (for example, historical justice or class justice) the neighbor is sometimes destroyed, killed, deprived of liberty, or stripped of fundamental human rights. The experience of the past and of our own time demonstrates that justice alone is not enough, that it can even lead to the negation and destruction of itself, if that deeper power, which is love, is not allowed to shape human life in its various dimensions. . . .
It only indicates, under another aspect, the need to draw from the powers of the spirit that condition the very order of justice powers that are still more profound. (197, p. 412)

Christians, formed by them [Christian churches], will bring to these human solutions a dimension that will enlighten the choice of goals and methods. They will, for example, be concerned about the small and the weak. Their honesty will not tolerate corruption. They will seek more just structures in the landed area. They will provide assistance, solidarity. They will seek to preserve in their community a brotherly and sisterly countenance. They will be artisans of peace. They will consider themselves managers of God's creation, which cannot be wasted or ravaged at will, for it is entrusted to human beings for the good of all. They will avoid the establishment of a materialism that would in fact be a slavery. In short, they want to work, from now on, for a world more worthy of the children of God. That is the role of lay Christians, helped by their pastors. (153, p. 23)

For believers, it is by allowing God to speak to human beings that one can contribute more truly to the strengthening of the consciousness that every human being has of his or her destiny, and to the awareness that all rights derive from the dignity of the person who is firmly rooted in God. . . .

While insisting—and rightly so—on the vindication of human rights, one should not lose sight of the obligations and duties that go with those rights. All individuals have the obligation to exercise their basic human rights in a responsible and ethically justified manner. Every man and woman has the duty to respect in others the rights claimed for themselves. Furthermore, we must contribute our share to the building up of a society that makes possible and feasible the enjoyment of rights and the discharge of duties inherent in those rights. (26, p. 417)

The state must ensure to all its members the possibility of a full development of their person. This requires that those who are in conditions of necessity and need owing to illness, poverty, or disablements of various kinds should be offered those services and those aids that their particular situation calls for. Even before being an obligation of justice on the part of the state, this is an obligation of solidarity on the part of each citizen.

For believers, furthermore, it is an irrepressible requirement of their faith in God the Father, who calls all to constitute a communion of brothers and sisters in Christ (cf. Mt 23:8–9). (18, p. 5)

All of humanity must think of the parable of the rich man and the beggar. Humanity must translate it into contemporary terms of economy and politics, in terms of all human rights, in terms of relations between the First, Second, and Third Worlds. We cannot stand idly by when thousands of human beings are dying of hunger. Nor can we remain indifferent when the rights of the human spirit are trampled upon, when violence is done to the human conscience in matters of truth, religion, and cultural creativity.

We cannot stand idly by, enjoying our own riches and freedom, if in any place the Lazarus of the twentieth century stands at our doors. In the light of the parable of Christ, riches and freedom mean a special responsibility. Riches and freedom create a special obligation. And so, in the name of the solidarity that binds all together in a common humanity, I again proclaim the dignity of every human being; the rich man and Lazarus are both human beings, both of them equally created in the image and likeness of God, both of them equally redeemed by Christ, at a great price, the price of "the precious blood of Christ" (1 Pt 1:19). (121, p. 312)

I Call Upon You to Sanctify Work

The value of work. Human beings can also love work for work's sake, because it enables them to take part in the great work of domination over the earth, a work that is planned by the creator. That love, it is true, corresponds to the dignity of humanity.

In the experience of my life, I have learned what a worker is, and I bear that in my heart. I know that work is also a necessity, sometimes a hard necessity, and yet all desire to transform it to the measure of their dignity and of their love. There lies their greatness. (158, p. 56)

Is enhanced by Jesus. With the central gift of Jesus Christ, the Church brings to the common work, not a prefabricated model, but a dynamic inheritance—doctrinal and practical—that developed in contact with the changing situations of this world, under the impulse of the gospel as the source of renewal, with a disinterested will for service and attention for the poorest (cf. Letter *Octagesima Adveniens*, no. 42). The whole Christian community takes part in this service. (12, p. 4)

The cross cannot be separated from human work. Christ cannot be separated from human work. . . . Christianity and the Church have no fear of the world of work. They have no fear of the system based on work. The Pope has no fear of people of work. They have always been particularly close to him. He has come from their midst. He has come from the quarries of Yakrzowek, from the Solvay furnaces in Borek Falecki, and then from Nowa Huta. Through all these surroundings, through his own experience of work, I make bold to say that the Pope learned the gospel anew. He noticed and became convinced that the problems being raised today about human labor are deeply engraved in the gospel, that they cannot be fully solved without the gospel. The problems being raised today (and is it really only today?) about human labor do not, in fact, come down in the last analysis—I say this with respect for all the specialists—either to technology or even to economics, but to a fundamental category: the category of the dignity of work, that is to say, of the dignity of the human being. Economics, technology, and the many other specializations and disciplines have their justification for existing in that single essential category. If they fail to draw from that category and are shaped without reference to the dignity of human labor, they are in error, they are harmful, they are against humanity.

This fundamental category is humanistic. I make bold to say that this fundamental category, the category of work as a measure of the dignity of the person, is Christian. We find it in its highest degree of intensity in Christ. (109, pp. 76–77)

However true it may be that the person is destined for work and called to it, in the first place work is for the person and not the person for work. Through this conclusion one rightly comes to recognize the preeminence of the subjective meaning of work over the objective one. Given this way of understanding things and presupposing that different sorts of work that people do can have greater or lesser objective value, let us try nevertheless to show that each sort is judged above all by the measure of the dignity of the subject of work, that is to say, the person, the individual who carries it out. On the other hand, independent of the work that every person does, and presupposing that this work constitutes a purpose—at times a very demanding one—of the person's activity, this purpose does not possess a definitive meaning in itself. In fact, in the final analysis it is always the person who is the purpose of the work, whatever work it is that is done by the person—even if the common scale of values rates it as the merest "service," as the most monotonous, even the most alienating work. (236, p. 230)

Laity must challenge its unjust aspects. I urge the implementation of social justice. Here, too, there are many problems, enormous ones, but I appeal to the conscience of everyone, employers and workers. Rights and duties are on both sides, and for society to be able to keep itself in the balance of peace and common prosperity, everyone must make an effort to fight and overcome selfishness. This is certainly a difficult undertaking, but Christians must make a point of being just in everything and with everyone, both in remunerating and protecting work and in spending their own strength. They must be, in fact, a witness to Christ everywhere and therefore also at work. (25, p. 7)

The Church considers it her duty to speak out on work from the viewpoint of its human value and of the moral order to which it belongs, and she sees this as one of her important tasks within the service that she renders to the evangelical message as a whole. At the same time she sees it as her particular duty to form a spirituality of work that will help all people to come closer, through work, to God, the creator and redeemer, to participate in his salvific plan for humanity and the world and to deepen their friendship with Christ in their lives by accepting, through faith, a living participation in his threefold mission as priest, prophet, and king, as the Second Vatican Council so eloquently teaches. (236, p. 241)

Develop a spirituality of work. The word of God's revelation is profoundly marked by the fundamental truth that human beings, created in the image of God, share by their work in the activity of the Creator and that within the limits of their own human capabilities, human beings in a sense continue to develop that activity and perfect it as they advance further and further in the discovery of the resources and values contained in the whole of creation. We find this truth at the very beginning of sacred scripture in the Book of Genesis, where the creation activity itself is presented in the form of "work" done by God during "six days," "resting" on the seventh day. Besides, the last book of sacred scripture echoes the same respect for what God has done through his creative "work" when it proclaims: "Great and wonderful are your deeds, O Lord God the Almighty"; this is similar to the Book of Genesis, which concludes the description of each day of creation with the statement: "And God saw that it was good."

This description of creation, which we find in the very first chapter of the Book of Genesis, is also in a sense the first "gospel of work." For it shows what the dignity of work consists of: it teaches that all people ought to imitate God, their creator, in working, because human beings alone have the unique characteristic of likeness to God. Individuals ought to imitate God both in working and also in resting, since God himself wished to present his own creative activity under the form of work and rest. This activity by God in the world always continues, as the words of Christ attest: "My Father is working still"; he works with creative power by sustaining in existence the world that he called into being from nothing, and he works with salvific power in the hearts of those whom from the beginning he has destined for "rest" in union with himself in his "Father's house." Therefore, human work too not only requires a rest every "seventh day," but also cannot consist in the mere exercise of human strength in external action; it must leave room for people to prepare themselves, by becoming more and more what in the will of God they ought to be, for the "rest" that the Lord reserves for his servants and friends. (236, pp. 241–242)

I call upon you to sanctify work. Work is not always easy, pleasant, satisfying; it may sometimes be heavy, not esteemed, not well paid, even dangerous. It is then necessary to remember that all work is collaboration with God to perfect the nature he created, and it is a service to brothers and sisters. It is necessary, therefore, to work with love and out of love! Then one will always be content and serene. (25, p. 7)

And offer the world a new perspective on life and worth. Without losing sight of the injustices that the workers suffer, I wanted to remind them that there existed "Good News," a "gospel of work," that is to say, that the vocation of human beings is to conquer the earth and to realize themselves as persons in this way. We shall never stop admiring, as we look across the centuries and the continents, the works, small and great, of people who were inventive, courageous, passionately fond of their work, and desirous of sharing the fruits of their labors.

There is another very astonishing aspect of this "gospel of work" that we should examine together. It is that of its mysterious value as a sharing in the redeeming work of Christ, through the silent offering of the fatigues that are part of work. Believing workers who unite themselves in spirit to Christ the Redeemer so ennoble their work that, through him, with him, and in him, it becomes a fatigue offered up for the love of God and of their brothers and sisters. Such hardships are life-giving.

Without this human and Christian vision of work, it is impossible to understand why readiness to work is a virtue. This, however, is what enables individuals to become more human, gives them the possibility of founding and supporting a family, and allows them to increase the heritage of their own country and of people everywhere in the world (cf. Encyclical *Laborem Exercens,* nos. 9–10, and Discourse at Saint-Denis, France, 31 May 1980). (263, p. 7)

The fundamental reason why I single out the theme of solidarity lies, therefore, in the very nature of human work. The problem of work has a very profound link with that of the meaning of human life. Because of this link, work becomes and indeed is a problem of human beings' spiritual nature. This observation in no way detracts from the other aspects of work, which one might say are more easily measurable and which are related to the various patterns and operations of an "external" character, arising out of the organization; this same observation indeed enables us to set human work, in whatever way it is performed by the person, within the person, in other words, in the person's innermost being, in the essence of the person's nature, in what makes the person human and therefore destined to work. The conviction that there is an essential link between the work of every person and the overall meaning of human existence is the whole foundation of the Christian doctrine of work—one might say the foundation of the "gospel of work"—and it permeates the teaching and activities of the Church, in one way or another, at each stage of its mission throughout history. "Never again will work be against the worker; but always work will be . . . in the service of humanity"—it is worth repeating today the words spoken in this same place in 1969 by Pope Paul VI (Address to ILO, 10 June 1969, no. 11, *Acta Apostolicae Sedis,* vol. 61, p. 495). If work must always serve the welfare of humanity, if the program of progress can only be carried out through work, then there is a fundamental right to judge progress in accordance with the following criterion: Does the work really serve humanity? Is it compatible with human dignity? Through it, does human life achieve fulfillment in all its richness and diversity?

We have the right to conceive of human work in this way; and we also have a duty to do so. We have the right and the duty to consider persons not according to whether or not they are useful in their work, but to consider work in its relation to human beings, to each person, to consider work according to whether or not it is useful to humanity. We have the right and the duty to take account, in our approach to work, of the various needs of human beings, in the spheres of both the spirit and the body, and to take this approach to human work in each society and in each system, in areas where well-being prevails, and even more so, in areas where destitution is widespread. We have the right and the duty to take this approach to work in its relation to humanity—and not the reverse—as a fundamental criterion for assessing progress itself. For progress always requires an evaluation and a value judgment: one must ask whether a given progress is sufficiently "human" and at the same time sufficiently "universal"; whether it helps to level out unjust inequalities and to promote a peaceful future for the world; whether, in the work itself, fundamental rights are ensured, for each person, for each family, and for each nation. In a word, one must constantly ask oneself whether the work helps to fulfil the meaning of human life. While seeking a reply to these questions when analyzing socioeconomic processes as a whole, one must not overlook the aspects and the content that form human beings' inner self: the development of their knowledge and their awareness. The link between work and the very meaning of human existence bears constant witness to the fact that human beings have not been alienated from work, that they have not been enslaved. Quite the contrary, it confirms that work has become the ally of their humanity, which helps them to live in truth and freedom, in a freedom built on truth that enables them to lead, in all its fullness, a life more worthy of human beings. (273, p. 11)

Dearest workers, employees, and directors. . . . I have listened with utmost attention to the addresses given by the spokespeople of the various components of your industrial complex. I picked out two clear elements in them: results and anxieties. The results have been achieved by you through the harmonious commitment, the generous dedication, and the firm hope that have supported you. But you also have anxieties about the difficult economic situation and the repercussions on your occupation that spring from it, whether in the immediate or distant future; anxieties about the tensions that disturb the country and about the outbursts of homicidal violence; anxieties, finally, about the threatening clouds that darken the international horizon because of the flagrant and often bloody violation of human rights, perpetrated in various parts of one or the other hemisphere.

I have listened to and appreciated the mature social conscience that was manifested in these addresses. What struck me in particular, besides the frank denunciation of a society "that renders humanity always more egoistic, always more alone, and always more dissatisfied," is the re-affirmed will to work for the building of a different world, in which "at the center of everything there is no longer profit and the thirst for power, but human beings with their needs for peace, democracy, and free-dom."

I am pleased with all of you, who have been well able to express the aspiration that inspires you in your daily commitment toward "an effective social justice and the respect for human dignity in the world of work." (264, p. 9)

CHAPTER 6

FAMILY LIFE

The Christian family is a small-scale Church.

The family is the fundamental cell of social life. It is created in the image and likeness of God and is blessed by Christ in the sacrament and becomes a Church in miniature—a domestic Church. Couples will maintain the values of family life and oppose and confront whatever might weaken its dignity.

Holiness of the family depends upon observance of the marriage promise.

Man and woman are a gift to each other, and their life together is their prime way of spiritual growth. They channel God's love to each other, and their sharing in faith brings Christ to their homes.

Jesus sent his disciples out two by two, and you are also sent in pairs.

Families are called to ministry. Their prime ministry is to witness to the Christian qualities of family life. Spouses share life with their children and receive love and hope. Their ministry becomes one of example and education within the family, and in cooperation with the Catholic schools, and challenge to unjust conditions in other families. Christian spouses will be sensitive to the vocational needs of the Church.

Sexuality is part of the total Christian ethos of redemption.

The meaning of human sexuality, sin and lust, transmission of life. The human body in its sexuality is in the image of God.

The Christian Family Is a Small-Scale Church

The family is the fundamental cell of social life. It is rightly said that the family is the fundamental cell of social life. It is the fundamental human community. Such as the family is, so is the nation, because so is humanity. I wish therefore that you may be strong, thanks to families profoundly rooted in the strength of God, and I wish that human beings may be able to fully develop themselves on the basis of the indissoluble bond of spouses-parents, in the family climate for which nothing can substitute. (106, p. 75)

That is why the family is irreplaceable and, as such, must be defended with might and main. Everything must be done in order that the family will not be replaced. That is necessary not only for the private good of every person, but also for the common good of every society, nation, and state. The family is set at the very center of common good in its various dimensions, precisely because each person is conceived and born in it. Everything possible must be done in order that this human being may be desired, awaited, experienced as a particular, unique, and unrepeatable value, right from the beginning, from the moment of conception. All must feel that they are important, useful, dear, and of great value, even if infirm or handicapped: even dearer, in fact, for this reason. This is the teaching that springs from the mystery of incarnation. (38, p. 10)

The solicitude of the Apostolic See and of the Episcopates of the whole world shone out brilliantly during the celebration of the Synod of Bishops in October of last year [1980]. At the end of the synod, I gathered up and developed its *Propositiones,* taking also into account the suggestions made at the daily meetings in which I took part. The result is the recent Apostolic Exhortation *Familiaris Consortio,* published a week ago, which sets out to be a "summa" of the teaching of the Church on the life, tasks, responsibilities, and mission of marriage and the family in the modern world.

In that document I recalled God's original plan for marriage, the visible expression of God's nuptial love for humanity, and of Christ's for the Church. The Christian family, which derives from marriage, is seen first of all in its component elements, with particular reference to the woman. Stress is laid on her indefeasible duty of service to life, both in the transmission of life itself and in her educational mission. The family must share deeply in the development of society and the work of the Church, as a community that believes, prays, and utters its "yes" to God in fulfilment of the law of love. The document finally considers various aspects of the family apostolate. It dwells also on difficult situations, typical of today, which, while respecting indispensable principles, need special attention—at once delicate and clear—for those involved in them.

This exhortation, which sums up the wishes and experience of the Episcopates of the five continents and is therefore a true expression of collegiality in the Church, confirms the solicitude of the Church for the family as an institution; furthermore, it is a deeper and fuller study of the clear teaching of the Second Vatican Council on marriage and the family (cf. Constitution *Gaudium et Spes,* nos. 47–52). (253, p. 9)

It is created in the image and likeness of God. It has been said, in a beautiful and profound way, that our God in his innermost mystery is not a solitary being, but a family, because he bears within himself fatherhood, sonship, and the essence of the family, which is love. This love in the Holy Family is the Holy Spirit. The subject of the family is not, therefore, foreign to the subject of the Holy Spirit. (53, p. 559)

God created human beings in his own image and likeness: calling them to existence through love, he called them at the same time for love.

God is love and in himself he lives a mystery of personal loving communion. Creating the human race in his own image and continually keeping it in being, God inscribed in the humanity of man and woman the vocation and thus the capacity and responsibility of love and communion. Love is therefore the fundamental and innate vocation of every human being. (250, p. 441)

The family finds in the plan of God the creator and redeemer not only its identity—what it is—but also its mission—what it can and should do. The role that God calls the family to perform in history derives from what the family is; its role represents the dynamic and existential development of what it is. Each family finds within itself a summons that cannot be ignored and that specifies both its dignity and its responsibility: Family, become what you are.

Accordingly, the family must go back to the "beginning" of God's creative act if it is to attain self-knowledge and self-realization in accordance with the inner truth, not only of what it is, but also of what it does in history. And since in God's plan it has been established as an "intimate community of life and love," the family has the mission to become more and more what it is, that is to say, a community of life and love in an effort that will find fulfilment, as will everything created and redeemed, in the kingdom of God. Looking at it in such a way as to reach its very roots, we must say that the essence and role of the family are in the final analysis specified by love. Hence, the family has the mission to guard, reveal, and communicate love, and this is a living reflection of and a real sharing in God's love for humanity and the love of Christ the Lord for the Church, his bride.

Every particular task of the family is an expression and concrete actuation of that fundamental mission. We must, therefore, go deeper into the unique riches of the family's mission and probe its contents, which are both manifold and unified.

Thus, with love as its point of departure and making constant reference to it, the recent synod emphasized four general tasks for the family: (1) forming a community of persons; (2) serving life; (3) participating in the development of society; and (4) sharing in the life and mission of the Church. (250, p. 443)

And is blessed by Christ in the sacrament. Dear brothers and sisters! On the indispensable foundation and premises of what has been said, we wish to turn now to the deepest mystery of marriage and the family. From the point of view of our faith, marriage is a sacrament of Jesus Christ. Love and conjugal fidelity are understood and sustained by the love and fidelity of God in Jesus Christ. The power of his cross and of his resurrection sustains and sanctifies Christian spouses.

As the recent Synod of Bishops stressed in its *Message to Christian Families in the Modern World,* the Christian family is called in particular to collaborate in God's salvific plan, since it helps its members "to become agents of the history of salvation and at the same time living signs of God's loving plan for the world" (Sec. III, n. 8).

As a "Church in miniature," sacramentally founded, or domestic Church, marriage and the family must be a school of faith and a place of common prayer. I attribute great significance precisely to prayer in the family. It gives strength to overcome the many problems and difficulties. In marriage and in the family the fundamental human and Christian attitudes, without which the Church and society cannot exist, must grow and mature. This is the first place for the Christian apostolate of the laity and of the common priesthood of all the baptized. Such marriages and families, imbued with the Christian spirit, are also the real seminaries, that is, seedbeds for spiritual vocations for the priestly and religious state.

Dear spouses and parents, dear families! What could I more heartily wish you on the occasion of today's Eucharistic meeting than this: That all of you and every single family may be such a "domestic Church," a Church in miniature! That the parable of the kingdom of God may be realized in you! That you may experience the presence of the Kingdom of God, in that you are yourselves a living "net" that unites and supports and gives refuge for yourselves and for many around you.

This is my good wish and blessing, which I express as your guest and pilgrim and as the servant of your salvation. (190, p. 2)

Certainly, every sacrament involves participation in Christ's nuptial love for his Church. But in marriage, the method and the content of this participation are specific. The spouses participate in it as spouses, together, as a couple, so that the first and immediate effort of marriage (*res et sacramentum*) is not supernatural grace itself, but the Christian conjugal bond, a typically Christian communion of two persons, because it represents the mystery of Christ's incarnation and the mystery of his covenant. The content of participation in Christ's life is also specific: conjugal love involves a totality, in which all the elements of the person enter: appeal of the body and instinct, power of feeling and affectivity, aspiration of the spirit and of will. It aims at a deeply personal unity, the unity that, beyond union in one flesh, leads to forming one heart and one soul; it demands indissolubility and faithfulness in definitive mutual giving; and it is open to fertility (cf. Encyclical *Humanae Vitae*, no. 9). In a word, it is certainly a question of the normal characteristics of all natural conjugal love, but with a new significance that not only purifies and strengthens them, but raises them to the extent of making them the expression of specifically Christian values. That is the perspective to which Christian spouses must rise; that is their grandeur, their strength, their exigency, and also their joy. (132, p. 15)

Marriage is a holy sacrament. Those baptized in the name of the Lord Jesus are married in his name also. Their love is a sharing in the love of God. He is its source. The marriages of Christian couples, today renewed and blessed, are images on earth of the wonder of God, the loving, life-giving communion of Three Persons in one God, and of God's covenant in Christ, with the Church.

Christian marriage is a sacrament of salvation. It is the pathway of holiness for all members of a family. With all my heart, therefore, I urge that your homes be centers of prayer; homes where families are at ease in the presence of God; homes to which others are invited to share hospitality, prayer, and the praise of God: "With gratitude in your hearts sing psalms and hymns and inspired songs to God; and never say or do anything except in the name of the Lord Jesus Christ, giving thanks to God the Father through him" (Col 3:16, 17).

In your country, there are many marriages between Catholics and other baptized Christians. Sometimes these couples experience special difficulties. To these families I say: You live in your marriage the hopes and difficulties of the path to Christian unity. Express that hope in prayer together, in the unity of love. Together invite the Holy Spirit of love into your hearts and into your homes. He will help you to grow in trust and understanding. (270, p. 9)

And becomes a Church in miniature—a domestic Church. Calling on the cooperation of all for missionary work, I would like to speak above all to the Christian family. In our day, we need to give back to the family, with its vitality and stability, its place of importance. What is true on the human level—that is, that the family is the basic cell of society, the foundation on which it is built—is also true of the Mystical Body of Christ, which is the Church; and for this reason the Council called the family "the domestic Church" (Dogmatic Constitution *Lumen Gentium,* no. 11). Thus the evangelization of the family is the principal aim of pastoral activity, and this will not attain its full scope if Christian families themselves do not become evangelizers and missionaries. (241, p. 1)

Insofar as it is a "small-scale Church," the Christian family is called upon, like the "large-scale Church," to be a sign of unity for the world and in this way to exercise its prophetic role by bearing witness to the kingdom and peace of Christ, toward which the whole world is journeying. (250, p. 453)

Couples will maintain the values of family life and oppose and confront whatever might weaken its dignity. The great danger for family life in the midst of any society whose idols are pleasure, comfort, and independence lies in the fact that people close their hearts and become selfish. The fear of making permanent commitments can change the mutual love of husband and wife into two loves of self—two loves existing side by side, until they end in separation.

In the sacrament of marriage, a man and a woman—who at baptism became members of Christ and hence have the duty of manifesting Christ's attitudes in their lives—are assured of the help they need to develop their love in a faithful and indissoluble union and to respond with generosity to the gift of parenthood. . . .

In order that Christian marriage may favor the total good and development of the married couple, it must be inspired by the gospel and thus be open to new life—new life to be given and accepted generously. The couple is also called to create a family atmosphere in which children can be happy and lead full and worthy human and Christian lives.

To maintain a joyful family requires much from both the parents and the children. Each member of the family has to become, in a special way, the servant of the others and share their burdens (cf. Gal 6:2; Phil 2:2). Each one must show concern, not only for his or her own life, but also for the lives of the other members of the family, their needs, their hopes, their ideals. (127, p. 279)

The Church is aware, in effect, that in these days the family confronts serious problems. . . . Recently, some countries have introduced divorce legislation that conveys a new menace to the integrity of the family. In the majority of your countries one grieves that an alarming number of children, hope of the future of these nations, are born in unstable homes, or as it is sometimes expressed, in "incomplete families." Furthermore, in certain places of the "Continent of Hope" this same hope runs the risk of being lost, because it grows in the womb of many families who cannot live normally because they must bear the most negative effects of development: depressing rates of disease, poverty, and misery; ignorance and illiteracy; inhuman housing conditions; chronic undernourishment; and so many other sorrowful realities. (53, p. 560)

The human body in its masculinity/femininity has almost lost the capacity of expressing this love, in which the person becomes a gift, in conformity with the deepest structure and finality of personal existence, as we have already observed in preceding analyses. If here we do not formulate this judgment absolutely and add the adverbial expression "almost," we do so because the dimension of the gift—namely, the capacity of expressing love with which a human being, by means of femininity or masculinity, becomes a gift for the other—has continued to some extent to permeate and mold the love that is born in the human heart. The nuptial meaning of the body has not become completely suffocated by concupiscence, but only habitually threatened.

The heart has become a battlefield between love and lust. . . . The image of the concupiscence of the body, which emerges from the present analysis, has a clear reference to the image of the person with which we connected our preceding reflections on the subject of the nuptial meaning of the body. Human beings indeed, as persons, are "the only creatures on earth that God has willed for their own sake" and, at the same time, they are the ones who "can fully discover their true self only in a sincere giving of themselves" (Constitution *Gaudium et Spes*, no. 24). Lust in general—and the lust of the body in particular—attacks precisely this "sincere giving." It deprives people, it could be said, of the dignity of giving, which is expressed by their bodies through femininity and masculinity, and in a way it depersonalizes human beings, making them objects for the other. Instead of being together with the other—a subject in unity, in fact, in the sacramental unity of the body—a person becomes an object for another person: the female for the male and vice versa. (172, p. 1)

The Church wishes to make her voice heard in support of elderly people, so well-deserving, but sometimes also so disregarded. So I repeat to you today what I had to say in November 1980, in Munich's Cathedral: "The Pope respectfully bows before the elderly and calls upon everyone to do so with him. Old age is a crowning of the stages of life. It bears the harvest of what has been learned and lived, the harvest of what has been carried out and reached, the harvest of what has been suffered and borne. As at the end of a great symphony, the dominant themes of life return for a powerful synthesis in sound. And this conclusive resonance confers wisdom . . . goodness, patience, understanding, love."

The old, therefore, are extremely precious, and, I would say, indispensable for the family and for society. How much help they are to young parents and their children with their knowledge and experience! Their advice and their action also benefit so many groups in which they, too, have their places and so many initiatives in the sphere of ecclesial and civil life. Let us all be grateful for this!

But they too, in their turn, need to be sustained and comforted in the difficulties in which they may find themselves because of health and loneliness. I express deep appreciation to all those persons who find the time and the way to approach and assist the elderly who are in most need because they are abandoned or forgotten in homes for the aged, which sometimes lack human warmth.

In particular, I address . . . a thought of gratitude and encouragement to the young, who dedicate themselves to spiritual and social assistance of the aged. It is a question of initiative taken either by individuals or by movements and organized associations, inspired by Christian faith, which makes us see the face of Jesus himself under the face of the person in need.

To all these young people I again express today my appreciation, my affection, and blessing them, I hope that they will continue in this meritorious and noble work of theirs. (255, p. 3)

Holiness of the Family Depends Upon the Observance of the Marriage Promise

Man and woman are a gift to each other. Human sexuality and personhood can be fully understood only when studied within the framework of the mystery of creation and the mystery of redemption. Following the example of Jesus (cf. Mt 19:4), we need to look at what God the Creator intended from the beginning. Thus in the Book of Genesis we read: "In the beginning . . . God created human beings in the image of himself, in the image of God he created them, male and female he created them" (Gn 1:1, 17). Examining the plan of God as it existed in the beginning we discover the nuptial meaning of the body; we see that, in the mystery of creation, man and woman are made to be a gift to each other and for each other. In their very existence, as male and female, by their sexuality and freedom as persons, man and woman are capable of mirroring the creative activity of God. And in the mystery of redemption, through the grace won by the Savior on the cross, man and woman receive not the power to return to the state of original innocence prior to the fall of Adam but the strength to live, in Christ and through Christ, a new ethos of redemptive love. (214, p. 5)

Do you know why I recall it [the marriage promise]? Because the "domestic Church," the quality and holiness of the family, the education of your children, depend on the observance of these commitments. Christ entrusted all that to you, beloved spouses, on the day in which he united your lives for ever, by means of the priest's ministry, at the moment in which you uttered the words that you must never forget: "until death do us part." If you remember them, if you observe them, beloved brothers and sisters, you are also apostles of Christ, and you contribute to the work of salvation (cf. Dogmatic Constitution *Lumen Gentium*, nos. 35, 41; Constitution *Gaudium et Spes*, no. 52). (21, p. 6)

And their life together is their prime way of spiritual growth.
To all I say, revere and protect your family and your family life, for the family is the primary field of Christian action. . . .

Married people must believe in the power of the sacrament to make them holy. They must believe in their vocation to witness through their marriage to the power of Christ's love. True love and the grace of God can never let marriage become a self-centered relationship of two individuals, living side by side for their own interests. (119, p. 325)

Marriage, one and indissoluble, as a human reality, is not something mechanical and static. Its success depends on the free cooperation of the spouses with the grace of God, on their response to his plan of love. If, owing to lack of cooperation with this divine grace, the union has remained deprived of its fruits, the spouses can and must bring back the grace of God, which the sacrament has ensured them, and renew their commitment to live a love that is one not only of affections and emotions but also, and above all, of dedication—mutual, free, voluntary, total, and irrevocable. (141, p. 700)

The family, instituted by God so that it might be the first and vital cell of human society, was so raised up by Christ the Redeemer, who deigned to be born into the family of Nazareth, that marriage, the intimate community of conjugal love and of life from which the family draws its origin, was elevated by him to the dignity of a sacrament in such a manner as to signify effectively the mystical bond of love between Christ and his Church (cf. Constitution *Gaudium et Spes*, no. 48).

In this sense, therefore, the Second Vatican Ecumenical Council described the family as a "domestic Church" (Dogmatic Constitution *Lumen Gentium*, no. 11; cf. also Decree *Apostolicam Actuositatem*, no. 11), showing thereby the particular role that the family is called to play in the entire plan of salvation and how demanding therefore is the duty that obliges the members of the family to actualize, each according to his or her own mission, the threefold prophetic, priestly, and kingly mission that Christ has confided to his Church. (232, p. 63)

Become what you are, "the first and vital cell of society. It is from the family that citizens come to birth, and it is within the family that they find the first school of the social virtues that are the animating principle of the existence and development of society itself" (Apostolic Exhortation *Familiaris Consortio*, no. 42). It is the family that takes each man and woman out of anonymity, and makes them conscious of their personal dignity, enriching them with deep human experiences and actively placing them, in their uniqueness, within the fabric of society.

Brothers and sisters, if you love your country, then love your family life. If you wish to avoid having a society that runs the risk of becoming more and more depersonalized and standardized and therefore inhuman and dehumanizing, then strengthen the structures of family life. Love your families. Respect them.

And you, young people, prepare yourselves for marriage by prayer, by self-discipline, mutual respect, and chastity. For the full and genuine gift of self can only take place in permanent married love. . . .

Your dignity and responsibility as disciples of Jesus come from the fact that you are called to be holy, and to help each other, the ecclesial community, and the world to become holy. Again we hear Saint Paul's words from the second reading: "Let the message of Christ in all its richness find home with you. Teach each other, and advise each other in all wisdom."

Become holy through God's gifts of faith, hope, and love, through personal and family prayer, through loving trust in our heavenly Father, through good example, through the life of grace nourished and sustained in the sacraments. Become holy by taking part in the life of the Church in your local communities, in your parishes, in your dioceses, with respect and love for your priests and bishops. Become holy in the "service of love"—the love of God and of your fellow human beings, especially your families. Become holy, and help make the life and the many activities of your social and national communities holy. (259, p. 4)

They channel God's love to each other. It is the task of the Christian community to proclaim forcefully, before present-day society, the joyful announcement of redeemed human love. Christ has "freed" man and woman for the possibility of loving each other in truth and fullness. The great danger for family life, in a society in which pleasure, comforts, and independence are idols, lies in the fact that men and women may be induced to close their hearts to such a possibility, resigning themselves to a "reduced ideal" of the life of the couple. The Christian community must contest a view of the conjugal relationship that instead of unreserved mutual dedication proposes the mere coexistence of two loves, concerned, when all is said and done, only with themselves. If Christian marriage—I said in the course of my pilgrimage in Africa—is comparable to a very high mountain that places spouses in the immediate vicinity of God, it must be recognized that its ascent calls for a great deal of time and effort. But is that a reason for suppressing or lowering this summit? (homily at the Mass for Families, Kinshasa, 3 May 1980).

It is necessary to help individual couples to interpret their love correctly and to strengthen their own convictions, by studying the intrinsic reasons that justify the Christian view of marriage and the family and grasping its deep connections with the essential requirements of a really human anthropology.

For this purpose the community must take its place beside the couple with the offering of concrete help along the way that it traverses, to arrive at ever fuller realization of the ideal glimpsed with that depth of intuition that love gives to the eyes of the heart. (195, p. 11)

It is, therefore, in conforming themselves to Christ, who delivered himself through love to his Church, that the spouses arrive, day after day, at the love of which the Gospel speaks to us: "Love one another, as I have loved you" and, more precisely, at the perfection of indissoluble union on all levels. The Christian spouses have promised to communicate to one another all that they are and all that they have. It is the boldest contract ever, and also the most marvelous!

The union of their bodies, willed by God himself as the expression of the even profounder communion of their minds and their hearts, carried out with as much respect as tenderness, renews the dynamism and the youth of their solemn commitment, of their first "yes." (150, p. 8)

Love for his wife as mother of their children and love for the children themselves are for the man the natural way of understanding and fulfilling his own fatherhood. Above all, where social and cultural conditions so easily encourage a father to be less concerned with his family, or at any rate less involved in the work of education, efforts must be made to restore socially the conviction that the place and task of the father in and for the family is of unique and irreplaceable importance. As experience teaches, the absence of a father causes psychological and moral imbalance and notable difficulties in family relationships, as does, in contrary circumstances, the oppressive presence of a father, especially where there still prevails the phenomenon of "machismo," or a wrong superiority of male prerogatives that humiliates women and inhibits the development of healthy family relationships. (250, p. 446)

With the creation of man and woman in his own image and likeness, God crowns and brings to perfection the work of his hands. He calls them to a special sharing in his love and in his power as creator and Father through their free and responsible cooperation in transmitting the gift of human life: "God blessed them, and God said to them, 'be fruitful and multiply, and fill the earth and subdue it.' "

Thus the fundamental task of the family is to serve life, to actualize in history the original blessing of the creator, that of transmitting by procreation the divine image from person to person.

Fecundity is the fruit and the sign of conjugal love, the reciprocal self-giving of the spouses: "While not making the other purposes of matrimony of less account, the true practice of conjugal love, and the whole meaning of the family life that results from it, has this aim: that the couple be ready with stout hearts to cooperate with the love of the creator and the savior, who through them will enlarge and enrich his own family day by day" (Constitution *Gaudium et Spes*, no. 50).

However, the fruitfulness of conjugal love is not restricted solely to the procreation of children, even understood in its specifically human dimension: it is enlarged and enriched by all those fruits of moral, spiritual, and supernatural life that the father and mother are called to hand on to their children, and through the children to the Church and to the world. (250, p. 447)

The family, in fact, having been instituted "from the beginning" by God, possesses a truth of its own to which we must continually return, and in the light of which we must judge every situation. To ask ourselves, therefore, if the family is a "community in communion" is equivalent to asking ourselves if the family is really and wholly carrying out God's plan for it.

Listening continually and faithfully to God's Word and treasuring all that the experience of humanity has perceived, the Church has been discovering more and more the divine plan that constitutes the underlying truth of every family. With particularly deep insight, my predecessor Paul VI, of venerated memory, expressed this truth concisely: "Husband and wife, through that mutual gift of themselves, which is specific and exclusive to them alone, seek to develop that kind of personal union in which they complement each other in order to cooperate with God in the generation and education of new lives" (Encyclical *Humanae Vitae*, no. 8).

The family is a "community in communion" when, above all, the conjugal community is the communion. As we read in the Book of Genesis (1:28), God created human beings in his image; calling them to existence out of love, he called them at the same time to love. Since God is love and human beings are created in his image, the vocation to love has been, so to speak, organically inscribed in this image, that is, in the humanity of human beings, whom God created male and female. And the realization of this image is the deep truth of conjugal communion, which makes family communion possible at the root.

With the vocation to love, in fact, there is inseparably connected the vocation to the gift of life. The Church has always taught this inseparable connection: conjugal love is the source of human life, and the gift of human life requires conjugal love at its origin. It is in the light of this relationship, set up by God, that we understand how the family community can be in communion only when it is the place where love generates life and life springs from love. Neither of these two realities, love and life, would be authentic if they were separated: conjugal love would not exist according to the whole measure of its truth, nor would human life have an origin worthy of its unique grandeur. In a word: the conjugal community would not be in full communion nor, consequently, would it be able to make the family community be in communion. (248, p. 5)

And their sharing in faith brings Christ to their homes. Follow Christ! You who are married: Share your love and your burdens with each other, respect the human dignity of your spouse, accept joyfully the life that God gives through you, make your marriage stable and secure for your children's sake. (120, p. 269)

Christ, in fact, is the light and salvation of families, of married couples, of young people, of children, and then also of all those who practice various professions. . . . But in order that everything may turn out well, without friction or conflicts, each one must be able to say to the Lord with humility and desire: "Thy word is a lamp to my feet and a light to my path" (Ps 119[118]:105). This is possible if parish life is lived together and thoroughly, each one receiving nourishment from all, and all contributing to the growth of each one. (210, p. 3)

Family prayer has its own characteristic qualities. It is prayer offered in common, husband and wife together, parents and children together. Communion in prayer is both a consequence of and a requirement for the communion bestowed by the sacraments of baptism and matrimony. . . .

Family prayer has for its very own object family life itself, which in all its varying circumstances is seen as a call from God and lived as a filial response to his call. Joys and sorrows, hopes and disappointments, births and birthday celebrations, wedding anniversaries of the parents, departures, separations, and homecomings, important and far-reaching decisions, the death of those who are dear, etc.—all of these mark God's loving intervention in the family's history. They should be seen as suitable moments for thanksgiving, for petition, for trusting abandonment of the family into the hands of their common Father in heaven. The dignity and responsibility of the Christian family as the domestic Church can be achieved only with God's unceasing aid, which will surely be granted if it is humbly and trustingly petitioned in prayer. (250, p. 456)

The effectiveness of the laity, and in particular of Christian families, to give to the world the witness of faith and love is conditioned by their spiritual dynamism. (97, p. 5)

Jesus Sent His Disciples Out Two by Two and You Are Also Sent in Pairs

Families are called to ministry. The family must be conscious of the mission of the Church and of its participation in this mission, not only to persevere in the Church and to draw from its spiritual resources, but also to constitute the Church in its fundamental dimension, like a "miniature Church" (domestic Church). (181, p. 259)

The Word of God announced in today's liturgy describes the duty that it is fitting that we propose to Christian families in the Church and in the modern world: consciousness of one's own mission, which comes from the saving mission of Christ and is fulfilled as a special service. This consciousness is fed by the Word of the living God and by the power of Christ's sacrifice. In this way the testimony of life is developed, capable of forming the life of others and of sanctifying others in truth. From this consciousness flows the good that alone "guards from the evil one." The duty of the family is altogether like the duty of he who in the Gospel said of himself: "As long as I was with them, I guarded them with your name which you gave me. . . . Not one of them was lost" (Jn 17:12).

Yes, the duty of each Christian family is to guard and preserve humanity itself. (181, pp. 259–260)

When Jesus first sent the disciples to proclaim the Good News, he sent them "two by two" (cf. Mk 6:7). You too are sent in pairs by that great sacrament, which, making you husband and wife, makes you at the same time witnesses to the Crucified and Risen Christ.

In the sacrament, in fact, you receive as Christians a new dignity, the dignity of husband and wife, and a new mission, that is, participation in the mission which is that of the whole People of God and which, in various ways, takes its place in the triple mission—tria munera—of Christ himself.

You must carry out this mission with your whole life, fulfilling it especially by means of witness. (230, p. 2)

Since, moreover, the family is "the first vital cell of society," as the Second Vatican Council said (Decree Apostolicam Actuositatem, no. 11), far from withdrawing into itself, it must open to the social environment that surrounds it. In this way the role that the family has in relation to society is clearly shown. In fact, the family is the first school of social life for its young members, and it is irreplaceable. Acting in this way, the family becomes the most effective instrument of humanization and personalization of a society that runs the risks of becoming more and more depersonalized and massified, and therefore inhuman and dehumanizing, with the negative consequences of so many forms of escapism, such as, for example, alcoholism, drugs, and even terrorism.

Moreover, families, alone or in a group, can and must dedicate themselves to multiple works of social service, especially for the sake of the poor, and their social task is also called to find its expression in the form of political intervention. In other words, families must be the first to work in order to ensure that the laws and institutions of the state will abstain from doing harm, but above all, that they will support and defend positively the rights and duties of the family. In this sense families must be more and more aware of being the protagonists of "family policy" and assume responsibility for changing society. They are also called to cooperate in a new international order. (257, p. 4)

Their prime ministry is to witness to the Christian quality of family life. Its [the Holy Family's] condition is similar to that of so many other families. It is the meeting place of our solidarity with every family, with every community of a man and a woman in which a new human being is born. It is a Family that does not remain only on the altars, as an object of praise and veneration, but through so many episodes well known to us from the Gospels of St. Luke and St. Matthew approaches, in a certain way, every human family. It takes over those deep, beautiful, and at the same time difficult problems that married and family life bring with it. . . .

The importance of these fundamental duties is very great from many points of view. Not only from the point of view of this concrete community, their family, but also from the point of view of every human community, every society, nation, state, school, profession, and environment. Everything depends, generally speaking, on how the parents and the family carry out their first and fundamental duties, on the way and to the extent to which they teach this creature—who, thanks to them, has become a human being, has obtained humanity—to be a human being. The family cannot be replaced in this. Everything must be done in order that the family should not be replaced. (39, p. 3)

On the one hand, in fact, there is a more lively awareness of personal freedom and greater attention to the quality of interpersonal relationships in marriage, to promoting the dignity of women, to responsible procreation, to the education of children. There is also an awareness of the need for the development of interfamily relationships, for reciprocal spiritual and material assistance, the rediscovery of the ecclesial mission proper to the family and its responsibility for the building of a more just society. On the other hand, however, signs are not lacking of a disturbing degradation of some fundamental values; a mistaken theoretical and practical concept of the independence of the spouses in relation to each other; serious misconceptions regarding the relationship of authority between parents and children; the concrete difficulties that the family itself experiences in the transmission of values; the growing number of divorces; the scourge of abortion; the ever-more frequent re-course to sterilization; the appearance of a truly contraceptive mentality. (250, p. 440)

Animated in its own inner life by missionary zeal, the church of the home is also called to be a luminous sign of the presence of Christ and of his love for those who are "far away," for families who do not yet believe and for those Christian families who no longer live in accordance with the faith that they once received. (250, p. 455)

Spouses share life with their children and receive love and hope. [Having children] will lead, in addition, to the fullest realization of their reciprocal love. By not living their union simply for themselves, in fact, but also for others, that is, for the children, they discover a new way of accord and mutual presence: the children become witnesses of their love, and each couple can recognize in them the deep presence of the other. (206, p. 528)

The Holy See thinks that we can also speak of the rights of children from the moment of conception and particularly of the right to life, for experience shows more and more that children need special protection, de facto and de jure even, before their birth.

Stress could thus be laid on the right of children to be born in a real family, for it is essential that they should benefit from the beginning from the joint contribution of the father and the mother, united in an indissoluble marriage.

Children must also be reared, educated, in their family, the parents remaining "primary and principally responsible" for their education. . . .

Actually, to speak of the rights of children is to speak of the duties of parents and educators, who remain in the service of children of their higher interests. But growing children must take part themselves in their own development, with responsibilities that correspond to their capac-ities; and care must be taken not to neglect to speak to them also of their own duties toward others and toward society. (40, p. 5)

Children are a source of hope. They speak to their parents of the purpose of their parents' lives, they represent the fruits of their parents' love. They also make it possible to think of the future. Parents live for their children; they work and toil for them. And not only in the family, but also in every society children make people think of the future. In children the nation sees its own future, just as the Church sees her own future in them.

And it is therefore a good thing that the current year [1979] is for the whole world the year of the child. Remembering that, I wish, together with you, to embrace with my thought all children, wherever they may be. Many of them, taking advantage of the holidays, are certainly staying at the various holiday resorts (at least as regards that part of the globe which is now summer). They are enjoying the fascination of nature, they are enjoying the water, the woods, the mountains. The heavenly Father lets them have a good rest. According to the model of the Son of God, may they grow "in wisdom and in stature, and in favor with God and human beings" (Lk 2:52). Let them not cease to reawaken in us human hope and also that hope of the kingdom of God, which Christ has opened for those who become like them (cf. Mt 18:3). May they help us to remember that the kingdom of God is in our midst (cf. Lk 17:20).

We will come back on other occasions to talking about children. (112, p. 2)

Their ministry becomes one of example. By virtue of their ministry of educating, parents are through the witness of their lives the first heralds of the gospel for their children. Furthermore, by praying with their children, by reading the Word of God with them and by introducing them deeply through initiation into the Body of Christ—both the eucharistic and the ecclesial body—they become fully parents, in that they are begetters not only of bodily life but also of the life that through the Spirit's renewal flows from the cross and resurrection of Christ. (250, p. 451)

It must be observed that the family is not only the object of evangelization and catechesis, it is also, and indeed above all, the fundamental subject of evangelization. This is gathered from the whole teaching of the Second Vatican Council about the People of God and the apostolate of the laity. This is the main field, as it were, in which the same teaching is put into practice, and consequently where the renewal of the Church according to the mind of the same Council is brought about. (29, p. 12)

As you know, the quality of relations between parents is decisive for the harmonious development of the children. A lack in this domain may weigh heavily on the whole life of a human being. The relations of children with their father and mother, of brothers and sisters with one another, will also have repercussions at the level of relations with schoolmates and of their whole life. Even relations with God are facilitated, or hindered, or alas, rendered nonexistent, by the style of parental relations. (187, p. 8)

And education within the family, and in cooperation with the Catholic schools. In the first place, catechesis in the family. In the first years of the child's life, the basis and foundation of the child's future are laid. For this reason parents must understand the importance of their task in this regard. By virtue of the sacraments of baptism and marriage they are the first catechists of their children. To educate, in fact, is to continue the act of generation. In this age God passes among us particularly "through the mediation of the family" (*General Catechetical Directory,* no. 79).

Children need to learn and to see parents who love each other, who respect God, who are able to explain the first truths of faith, who are able to present the "content of Christianity" in the witness and endurance of "a day-to-day life lived in accordance with the gospel" (*Catechesi Tradendae,* nos. 36, 68).

Witness is fundamental. The Word of God is effective in itself, but it takes on concrete meaning when it becomes a reality in the person who proclaims it. (167, p. 5)

It is a question of helping children and adolescents "to make sound moral judgments and to put them into practice with a sense of personal commitment, and to know and love God more perfectly" (Declaration *Gravissimum Educationis,* no. 1). This education of their discernment, their will, and their faith is a whole art. The family atmosphere must be one of trust, dialogue, firmness, rightly understood respect of incipient freedom: all things that permit gradual initiation to meeting the Lord and to habits that already honor the child and prepare the person of tomorrow. May your children acquire in your families "their first experience of a well-balanced human society and of the Church" (Declaration *Gravissimum Educationis,* no. 3). It will be up to you, too, to introduce them gradually into educative communities wider than the family. The latter must then accompany its adolescents with patient love, in hope, and without resigning its task, cooperate with other educators. In this way, strengthened in their Christian identity to face in the right way a pluralistic world, often indifferent or even hostile to their convictions, these young people will be able to become strong in faith, serve society, and take an active part in the life of the Church in communion with their pastors, and putting into application the orientations of the Second Vatican Council. (8, p. 12)

The submission, obedience, readiness to accept the mature examples of the human conduct of the family, is necessary on the part of children and of the young generation. Jesus, too, was "obedient" in this way. And parents must measure their whole conduct with this obedience, this readiness of the child to accept the example of human behavior. This is the particularly delicate point of their responsibility as parents, of their responsibility with regard to the person, this little and then growing person entrusted to them by God himself. (35, p. 4)

In the face of contempt for the supreme value of life, which goes so far as to ratify the suppression of the human being in the mother's womb; in the face of the disintegration of family unity, the only guarantee for the complete formation of children and young people; in the face of the devaluation of clear and pure love, unbridled hedonism, the spread of pornography, it is necessary to recall emphatically the holiness of marriage, the value of the family, the inviolability of human life. (202, p. 496)

The family's catechetical activity has a special character, which is in a sense irreplaceable. This special character has been rightly stressed by the Church, particularly by the Second Vatican Council. Education in the faith by parents, which should begin from the children's tenderest age, is already being given when the members of a family help each other to grow in faith through the witness of their Christian lives, a witness that is often without words but that perseveres throughout a day-to-day life lived in accordance with the gospel. . . .

Family catechesis therefore precedes, accompanies, and enriches all other forms of catechesis. . . . Thus, there cannot be too great an effort on the part of Christian parents to prepare for this ministry of being their own children's catechists and to carry it out with tireless zeal. (129, p. 345)

The sacrament of marriage gives to the educational role the dignity and vocation of being really and truly a "ministry" of the Church at the service of the building up of her members. So great and splendid is the educational ministry of Christian parents that St. Thomas has no hesitation in comparing it with the ministry of priests: "Some only propagate and guard spiritual life by a spiritual ministry: this is the role of the sacrament of orders; others do this for both corporal and spiritual life, and this is brought about by the sacrament of marriage, by which a man and a woman join in order to beget offspring and bring them up to worship God."

A vivid and attentive awareness of the mission that they have received with the sacrament of marriage will help Christian parents to place themselves at the service of their children's education with great serenity and trustfulness, and also with a sense of responsibility before God, who calls them and gives them the mission of building up the Church in their children. Thus, in the case of baptized people, the family, called together by word and sacrament as the church of the home, is both teacher and mother, the same as the worldwide Church. (250, p. 450)

The family has the first and fundamental right to educate; but it also has the duty to educate. In fulfilling this essential duty, which strictly pertains to its vocation, the family drinks from the fountains of culture, which is the great treasure of all humanity; and more directly, from the culture of the environment in which it is rooted. Because of this order of fact, human beings become heirs of the past, which in them becomes transformed into the future: not only the future of their own family, but also of their nation and of all humanity.

At the same time that this normal cycle of the family is going on, the cycle of the birth and education of the human being, the divine plan of salvation organically passes through the person made to human measure right from the beginning, together with the union of marriage, and confirmed and renewed—after the fall into sinfulness—in Jesus Christ. The divine plan of salvation reaches its fullness in Jesus Christ. (268, p. 4)

The issues focused on above, especially the development of the whole person, the spiritual dimension of education, and the involvement of parents, have always been central to the ethos of the Catholic school. This has been particularly true of the primary school, with the close bond between the family, school, parish, and local community. Nor has this been absent in the more complex situation of the secondary sector, where the diocese often provides chaplains, above all for the school as a community of faith centered on the Eucharist and also, where possible, to serve as a pastoral link with the local parishes. However, always mindful of the constant need for improvement, the Catholic school ought to make full use of suitable new opportunities available, for no other reason than to fulfil its own identity and role. And we do well at this point to recollect what precisely is the identity and purpose of the Catholic school.

Such a reminder is conveniently provided in the document of that title, "The Catholic School," published by the Holy See's Sacred Congregation for Christian Education in March 1977: "The Catholic school," it declares, "is committed . . . to the development of the whole person, since in Christ, the perfect human being, all human values find their fulfilment and unity. Herein lies the specifically Catholic character of the school. Its duty to cultivate human values in their own legitimate right in accordance with its particular mission to serve all people has its origin in the figure of Christ. . . . Its task is fundamentally a synthesis of culture and faith and a synthesis of faith and life (pp. 35–37). (271, p. 14)

And challenge to unjust conditions in other families. For you, the families that are able to enjoy material comfort: don't be selfish with your happiness. Be open to the others and share with them what you have and they lack. Families oppressed by poverty, don't get discouraged. Without making luxury your objective or making wealth the principle of happiness, search with the help of all to overcome the difficult times in the hope of better days. Families tried by any physical or moral sorrow, such as sickness or misery, do not add bitterness or desperation to such sufferings, but defeat sorrow with hope. (52, p. 5)

Along these lines families should grow in awareness of being protagonists of what is known as "family politics" and assume responsibility for transforming society; otherwise, families will be the first victims of the evils that they have done no more than note with indifference. (250, p. 452)

Experience confirms that there must be a social reevaluation of the mother's role, of the toil connected with it, and of the need that children have for care, love, and affection in order that they may develop into responsible, morally and religiously mature, and psychologically stable persons. It will redound to the credit of society to make it possible for a mother—without inhibiting her freedom, without psychological or practical discrimination, and without penalizing her as compared with other women—to devote herself to taking care of her children and educating them in accordance with their needs, which vary with age. Having to abandon these tasks in order to take up paid work outside the home is wrong, from the point of view of the good of society and of the family, when it contradicts or hinders these primary goals of the mission of a mother. (236, p. 239)

Christian spouses will be sensitive to the vocational needs of the Church. The Christian family is also supremely vital for vocations to the priesthood and the religious life. The majority of such vocations spring to life and develop in deeply Christian families. . . .

I am certain too that the numerous vocations within the "little flock" of the Catholic community . . . are born and grow within families animated by a spirit of faith, charity, and piety. . . .

I exhort every Christian family . . . to be truly a "church of the home": a place where God is given thanks and praise, a place where his Word is listened to and his law obeyed, a place where education is given for faith and where faith is fostered and strengthened, a place of fraternal charity and mutual service, a place of openness to others, especially the poor and the needy. (222, p. 638)

But the contribution of the family is necessary to bring a vocation to maturity. In the recent exhortation on the role of the Christian family in the modern world, I wrote that it is "the primary and most excellent seedbed of vocations to a life of consecration to the Kingdom of God"; in fact, "the service rendered by Christian spouses and parents to the gospel is essentially an ecclesial service. It has its place within the context of the whole Church as an evangelized and evangelizing community" (Apostolic Exhortation *Familiaris Consortio,* no. 53).

Dear parents here present, I earnestly exhort you to continue more and more to be among the men and women who deeply feel the problems of the life of the Church, who shoulder these problems and are also able to transmit this sensitivity to their children, with prayer, reading of the Word of God, and living example. Normally, a vocation is born and matures in a healthy, responsible, and Christian family background. It becomes rooted precisely there and draws from it the possibility of growing and becoming a strong tree, laden with ripe fruit. (251, p. 5)

By making use of the creative collaboration of the parents, God the Father wishes to repeat once more his call to new descendants of the human race. He wants to call them, too, to become "co-heirs of God's promise" and to start toward the "land" that was "promised" in Jesus Christ to all humanity.

The family is the place of the person's divine vocation. It is necessary that Christian couples and parents be conscious of this responsibility and that they do their best to collaborate with this divine vocation of the new person, developing the work of Christian education, above all with that catechesis that springs from living example.

Vocations, particularly important to the Church's salvific mission, are also born in Christian families, cradle of future priests, religious, missionaries, and apostles! Although difficulties exist in the educational structure, Christian parents must, with faith and courage, educate their children in the essential values of human life, without ever losing sight of the fact that being responsible for the domestic Church of their households, they are called to build up the great Church in their children (cf. Apostolic Exhortation *Familiaris Consortio,* no. 38) and, who knows, to build it up through their children "called by God." And if God does, in fact, call them to the service of his Kingdom, dear fathers and mothers, be generous to him, as he has been to you. (268, p. 5)

Sexuality Is Part of the Total Christian Ethos of Redemption

The meaning of human sexuality. By virtue of the covenant of married life, the man and woman "are no longer two but one flesh" and they are called to grow continually in their communion through day-to-day fidelity to their marriage promise of total mutual self-giving.

This conjugal communion sinks its roots in the natural complementarity that exists between man and woman and is nurtured through the personal willingness of the spouses to share their entire life project, what they have and what they are: for this reason such communion is the fruit and the sign of a profoundly human need. But in the Lord Christ God takes up this human need, confirms it, purifies it, and elevates it, leading it to perfection through the sacrament of matrimony: the Holy Spirit who is poured out in the sacramental celebration offers Christian couples the gift of a new communion of love that is the living and real image of that unique unity that makes of the Church the indivisible mystical body of the Lord Jesus. (250, p. 444)

The physical and at the same time spiritual nature of conjugal communion, always enlightened by personal love, must lead to respect for sexuality, its fully human dimension, and never to use it as an object, in order not to dissolve the personal union of soul and body, striking "at the deepest interaction of nature and person" (Apostolic Exhortation *Familiaris Consortio*, no. 32). The responsibility for the generation of human life— the life that must be born in a family—is great before God! (268, p. 5)

An examination of moral norms and a quest for appropriate pastoral approaches to the various problems of human sexuality would be incomplete if reference were not made to the teachings of Christ found in the Sermon on the Mount, especially to the Lord's words: "You have heard that it was said, 'You shall not commit adultery.' But I say to you that everyone who looks at a woman lustfully has already committed adultery with her in his heart" (Mt 5:27). As we examine this teaching, which reminds us of the importance of purity of heart, as well as the need for lifelong fidelity to one's spouse, we must continually recall that the words of our Savior are not words of accusation or condemnation. Rather, they are words of invitation, words of truth spoken in love and compassion, words that lead men and women to the fullness of life and freedom. For they invite men and women to live in accordance with the truth of their own personhood and sexuality as revealed by God from the beginning. We, on our part, must help our people to see moral teaching on sexuality as part of the total Christian ethos of redemption, as part of their calling in Christ to "walk in newness of life" (Rom 6:4). All pastoral charity that is authentic, all human compassion that is genuine, all fraternal support that is real, embraces and communicates the whole truth as revealed to us by the eternal Word and proclaimed by his Church. (214, p. 5)

As an incarnate spirit, that is, a soul that expresses itself in a body and a body informed by an immortal spirit, each one is called to love in his or her unified totality. Love includes the human body, and the body is made a sharer in spiritual love.

Christian revelation recognizes two specific ways of realizing the vocation of the human being, in its entirety, to love: marriage and virginity or celibacy. Either one is in its own proper form an actuation of the most profound truth of the human being, of being "created in the image of God."

Consequently, sexuality, by means of which man and woman give themselves to one another through the acts that are proper and exclusive to spouses, is by no means something purely biological, but concerns the innermost being of the human being as such. It is realized in a truly human way only if it is an integral part of the love by which a man and a woman commit themselves totally to one another until death. The total physical self-giving would be a lie if it were not the sign and fruit of a total personal self-giving, in which the whole person, including the temporal dimension, is present: If the person were to withold something or reserve the possibility of deciding otherwise in the future, by this very fact he or she would not be giving totally. (250, p. 441)

Sin and lust. The faithful do not always remain immune from the obscuring of certain fundamental values. . . . Among the more troubling signs of this phenomenon, the synod fathers stressed the following, in particular: the spread of divorce and of recourse to a new union, even on the part of the faithful; the acceptance of purely civil marriage in contradiction to the vocation of the baptized to "be married in the Lord"; the celebration of the marriage sacrament without living faith, but for other motives; the rejection of the moral norms that guide and promote the human and Christian exercise of sexuality in marriage. (250, p. 440)

History, which began so well in the luminous dawn of the human race, knew the drama of the rupture between the newly created couple and the creator. That is original sin. Nevertheless, this rupture will be the occasion for a new manifestation of the love of God. Compared very often to an infinitely faithful spouse, for example, in the texts of the psalmists and the prophets, God reforms incessantly his alliance with capricious and sinful humanity. (150, p. 8)

You know as well as I do how much the notions of fidelity and indissolubility are disparaged by public opinion. You know also that the fragility and break-up of families give rise to a string of miseries. . . . Christian homes—solidly prepared and duly assisted—have to work without discouragement for the restoration of the family, which is the first cell of society and must remain a school of social virtues. The state must not fear such homes but must protect them. (150, p. 9)

Concupiscence "that comes from the world"—here it is directly a question of the concupiscence of the body—limits and distorts the body's objective way of existing, of which man and woman have become participants.

The human "heart" experiences the degree of this limitation or distortion, especially in the sphere of man-woman mutual relations. Precisely in the experience of the "heart," femininity and masculinity, in their mutual relations, no longer seem to be the expression of the spirit that aims at personal communion, and remain only an object of attraction, in a certain sense as happens "in the world" of living beings that, like human beings, have received the blessing of fertility (cf. Gn 1). (172, p. 1)

Transmission of life. Marriage must include openness to the gift of children. Generous openness to accept children from God as the gift to their love is the mark of the Christian couple. Respect the God-given cycle of life, for this respect is part of our respect for God himself, who created male and female, who created them in his own image, reflecting his own life-giving love in the patterns of their sexual being.

And so I say to all, have an absolute and holy respect for the sacredness of human life from the first moment of its conception. Abortion, as the Vatican Council stated, is one of the "abominable crimes" (Constitution *Gaudium et Spes*, no. 51).

To attack unborn life at any moment from its conception is to undermine the whole moral order that is the true guardian of the well-being of humanity. The defense of the absolute inviolability of unborn life is part of the defense of human rights and human dignity. (119, p. 325)

Precisely because the love of husband and wife is a unique participation in the mystery of life and of the love of God himself, the Church knows that she has received the special mission of guarding and protecting the lofty dignity of marriage and the most serious transmission of human life.

Thus, in continuity with the living tradition of the ecclesial community throughout history, the recent Second Vatican Council and the magisterium of my predecessor Paul VI, expressed above all in the encyclical *Humanae Vitae,* have handed on to our times a truly prophetic proclamation, which reaffirms and reproposes with clarity the Church's teaching and norm, always old yet always new, regarding marriage and regarding the transmission of human life.

For this reason the synod fathers made the following declaration at their last assembly: "This sacred synod, gathered together with the successor of Peter in the unity of faith, firmly holds what has been set forth in the Second Vatican Council (cf. Constitution *Gaudium et Spes,* no. 50) and afterward in the encyclical *Humanae Vitae,* particularly that love between husband and wife must be fully human, exclusive, and open to new life (Encyclical *Humanae Vitae,* no. 11; cf. nos. 9, 12)." (250, p. 447)

I do not hesitate to proclaim before you and before the world that all human life—from the moment of conception and through all subsequent stages—is sacred, because human life is created in the image and likeness of God.

Nothing surpasses the greatness or dignity of a human being. Human life is not just an idea or an abstraction. Human life is the concrete reality of a being that lives, that acts, that grows and develops. Human life is the concrete reality of a being that is capable of love and of service to humanity. . . .

Human life is precious because it is the gift of a God whose love is infinite; and when God gives life, it is for ever. Life is also precious because it is the expression and the fruit of love. This is why life should spring up within the setting of marriage and the partners' love for one another should be marked by generosity in self-giving. (127, p. 279)

The human body in its sexuality is in the image of God. It is the task of the Christian community to proclaim forcefully, before present-day society, the joyful announcement of redeemed human love. Christ has "freed" man and woman for the possibility of loving each other in truth and fullness. The great danger for family life, in a society in which pleasure, comforts, and independence are idols, lies in the fact that men and women may be induced to close their hearts to such a possibility, resigning themselves to a "reduced ideal" of the life of the couple. The Christian community must contest a view of the conjugal relationship that instead of unreserved mutual dedication proposes the mere coexistence of two loves, concerned, when all is said and done, only with themselves. (195, p. 11)

Everyone is familiar with the famous story of creation by which the Bible begins. It is said there that God made human beings in his likeness in creating them man and woman. There is something surprising right away. Humankind, to resemble God, must be a couple, two persons in movement toward one another, two persons whom a perfect love is going to unite. This movement and this love make them resemble God who is love itself, the absolute unity of three persons. Never has anyone sung so beautifully of the splendor of human love as in the first pages of the Bible: " 'This one,' " says Adam in contemplating his wife, 'is flesh of my flesh, bone of my bones.' That is why man will leave his father and mother and cling to his wife and they shall be but one flesh" (Gn 2:23–24). (150, p. 8)

Conjugal communion is characterized not only by its unity but also by its indissolubility: "As a mutual gift of two persons, this intimate union, as well as the good of children, imposes total fidelity on the spouses and argues for an unbreakable oneness between them. . . ." (Constitution *Gaudium et Spes,* no. 48)

Being rooted in the personal and total self-giving of the couple and being required by the good of the children, the indissolubility of marriage finds its ultimate truth in the plan that God has manifested in his revelation: He wills and he communicates the indissolubility of marriage as a fruit, a sign, and a requirement of the absolutely faithful love that God has for humanity and that the Lord Jesus has for the Church. (250, p. 444)

I say to all married couples and to parents, young and adult: take each other's hand as you did on your wedding day, on receiving the sacrament of marriage joyfully. Imagine your bishop asking you again today for your consent and yourselves uttering, as then, the words of the marriage promise, the oath of your marriage.

Do you know why I recall it? Because the "domestic Church," the quality and holiness of the family, the education of your children, depend on the observance of these commitments. (21, p. 7)

SERMONS AND ADDRESSES BY JOHN PAUL II
CITED IN THE TEXT

1. "First Address as the Bishop of Rome to the World," 17 October 1978. *L'Osservatore Romano* 552, no. 43 (26 October 1978): 3–4.
2. "Diplomatic Corps," 20 October 1978. *L'Osservatore Romano* 553, no. 44 (2 November 1978): 3.
3. "Address to the International Press," 20 October 1978. *L'Osservatore Romano* 553, no. 44 (2 November 1978): 3–4.
4. "The Inauguration Homily," 22 October 1978. *Origins* 8 (1978): 305–308.
5. "Message to the Catholic International Association of Radio and Television on Its 50th Anniversary," 25 October 1978. *L'Osservatore Romano* 554, no. 45 (9 November 1978): 9, 12.
6. "Address to the International Council of Catholic Men," 28 October 1978. *L'Osservatore Romano* 554, no. 45 (9 November 1978): 4.
7. "Address on Prayer to the Faithful at Marian Sanctuary of Mentorella, Mount Guadagnolo," 29 October 1978. *L'Osservatore Romano* 554, no. 45 (9 November 1978): 1.
8. "Address to the Participants in the Third International Congress on the Family," 30 October 1978. *L'Osservatore Romano* 554, no. 45 (9 November 1978): 2, 12.
9. "Message to the President of the International Catholic Film Organization on Its 50th Anniversary," 31 October 1978. *L'Osservatore Romano* 556, no. 47 (23 November 1978): 4.
10. "Address at the Shrine of St. Catherine of Siena Concerning Awareness of the Christian Vocation," 5 November 1978. *L'Osservatore Romano* 555, no. 46 (16 November 1978): 6–7.
11. "Youth," General Audience, Rome, 8 November 1978. *L'Osservatore Romano* 555, no. 46 (16 November 1978): 1.
12. "Justice and Peace," Pontifical Commission, 11 November 1978. *L'Osservatore Romano* 557, no. 48 (30 November 1978): 4.
13. "Address to the Crowd in St. Peter's Square at the Angelus," 12 November 1978. *L'Osservatore Romano* 556, no. 47 (23 November 1978): 2.

14. "Only Love Constructs," homily on taking possession of his see as Bishop of Rome, Archbasilica of St. John Lateran, 12 November 1978. *L'Osservatore Romano* 556, no. 47 (23 November 1978): 7.
15. "Fortitude," Audience for youth, Rome, 15 November 1978. *L'Osservatore Romano* 556, no. 47 (23 November 1978): 1, 9.
16. "Precious Service in the Community," address to the Fire Brigade Cadets, Rome, 15 November 1978. *L'Osservatore Romano* 556, no. 47 (23 November 1978): 12.
17. "Temperance," General Audience, 22 November 1978. *L'Osservatore Romano* 557, no. 48 (30 November 1978): 2.
18. "Address to the Union of Italian Catholic Jurists," 25 November 1978. *L'Osservatore Romano* 558, no. 49 (7 December 1978): 5.
19. "Full Ecclesial Communion in a Spirit of True Charity," address to bishops to Honduras, 25 November 1978. *L'Osservatore Romano* 558, no. 49 (7 December 1978): 4.
20. "To Serve Mankind in Order to Be in Solidarity With Christ," Catholic Laity of Rome, 26 November 1978. *L'Osservatore Romano* 558, no. 49 (7 December 1978): 10.
21. "Address to Parishioners of St. Francis Xavier's Church, Garbatella," 3 December 1978. *L'Osservatore Romano* 559, no. 50 (14 December 1978): 6–7.
22. "Service of God and Man," Catholic University of the Sacred Heart, 8 December 1978. *L'Osservatore Romano* 560, no. 51 (21 December 1978): 9–10.
23. "Receiving the Credentials of the Ambassador of Nicaragua." *L'Osservatore Romano* 561, no. 52 (28 December 1978): 7.
24. "Address to the Apostolic Movement of the Blind, 50th Anniversary," 9 December 1978. *L'Osservatore Romano* 561, no. 52 (28 December 1978): 4.
25. "Address to Christian Workers," Rome, 9 December 1978. *L'Osservatore Romano* 561, no. 52 (28 December 1978): 4, 7.
26. "An Appeal for Religious Freedom," United Nations, on the anniversary of the Universal Declaration of Human Rights, 11 December 1978. *Origins* 8 (1978): 417, 419–420.
27. "The Gospel as Part of the Way of Life of the Irish People," address to the Ambassador from Ireland, 12 December 1978. *L'Osservatore Romano* 560, no. 51 (21 December 1978): 4.
28. "Discourse to the Minister of Foreign Affairs of Bulgaria," 13 De-

cember 1978. *L'Osservatore Romano* 561, no. 52 (28 December 1978): 2.

29. "Role of the Family in Today's World," Synod of Bishops, 16 December 1978. *L'Osservatore Romano* 562, no. 1 (1 January 1979): 12.

30. "Christmas Address," 22 December 1978. *Origins* 8 (1979): 449–453.

31. "Address to the Catholic Action Youth [Italian]," 23 December 1978. *L'Osservatore Romano* 563, no. 2 (8 January 1979): 4.

32. "Christmas Message, Urbi et Orbi," 25 December 1978. *Origins* 8 (1979): 454–455.

33. "Address to the Federation of Institutes of Educational Activities, F.I.D.A.E.," Rome, 29 December 1978. *L'Osservatore Romano* 563, no. 2 (8 January 1979): 12.

34. "Address to the Members of Italian Catholic Action," 30 December 1978. *L'Osservatore Romano* 563, no. 2 (8 January 1979): 8, 12.

35. "Fundamental Family Values," homily at the Church of the Gesu, 31 December 1979. *L'Osservatore Romano* 564, no. 3 (15 January 1979): 4.

36. "Letter to Cardinal Knox and the Committee for the International Eucharistic Congresses," 1 January 1979. *L'Osservatore Romano* 570, no. 9 (26 February 1979): 9–10.

37. "World Day of Peace Message," 1 January 1979. *Origins* 8 (1979): 455–460.

38. "The Family at the Center of Society's Well-Being," General Audience, 3 January 1979. *L'Osservatore Romano* 563, no. 2 (8 January 1979): 10.

39. "Love and Respect for Nascent Life," General Audience, 3 January 1979. *L'Osservatore Romano* 563, no. 2 (8 January 1979): 3.

40. "Protect Childhood for the Good of Society," 13 January 1979. *L'Osservatore Romano* 565, no. 4 (22 January 1979): 5.

41. "Man's Answer to God's Call to Service," homily at St. Mary Liberator, Monte Testaccio, 14 January 1979. *L'Osservatore Romano* 565, no. 4 (22 January 1979): 3.

42. "Learn to Overcome Evil With Good," Angelus Message, 21 January 1979. *L'Osservatore Romano* 566, no. 5 (29 January 1979): 2.

43. "Establishing Communion With Priests and Laity," Italian Bishops Conference, 23 January 1979. *Origins* 8 (1979): 602–603.

44. "Ministry, Evangelization," Italian Episcopal Conference, 23 January 1979. *L'Osservatore Romano* 569, no. 8 (19 February 1979): 9; also in *Origins* 8 (1979): 602–603.

45. "Address on Arrival in the Dominican Republic on Evangelization," 25 January 1979. *L'Osservatore Romano* 567, no. 6 (5 February 1979): 8–9.

46. "Proclamation of the Gospel and Human Advancement," homily, Independence Square, Dominican Republic, 25 January 1979. *L'Osservatore Romano* 567, no. 6 (5 February 1979): 8–9.

47. "Homily, Santo Domingo," 25 January 1979. *Origins* 8 (1979): 542–543.

48. "I See You in the Suffering Lord," greeting to the poor of Los Minas, Dominican Republic," 26 January 1979. *L'Osservatore Romano* 576, no. 6 (5 February 1979): 10.

49. "Address to the Mexican Diplomatic Corps," 26 January 1979. *L'Osservatore Romano* 568, no. 7 (12 February 1979): 2–3.

50. "A Call to Fidelity," homily, Mexico City, 26 January 1979. *Origins* 8 (1979): 541–542.

51. "Opening Address to the Third General Assembly of the Latin American Bishops in Puebla, Mexico," 28 January 1979. *Origins* 8 (1979): 531–538.

52. "Homily to the People of Puebla," 28 January 1979. *L'Osservatore Romano* 568, no. 7 (12 February 1979): 5.

53. "The Family: Hope of Latin America," homily at Puebla, 28 January 1979. *Origins* 8 (1979): 559–560.

54. "Address to the Representatives of the Catholic Organizations of Mexico," 29 January 1979. *L'Osservatore Romano* 568, no. 7 (12 February 1979): 6.

55. "Address to the Rural Poor of Cuilapan, Mexico," 29 January 1979. *Origins* 8 (1979): 543–544.

56. "Homily in Oaxaca Cathedral," 29 January 1979. *L'Osservatore Romano* 568, no. 7 (12 February 1979): 8–9.

57. "Address to the Catholic Students at Guadalajara, Mexico," 30 January 1979. *L'Osservatore Romano* 568, no. 7 (12 February 1979): 8.

58. "Evangelization and Social Involvement," homily at the Basilica of Our Lady of Zapopan, Mexico, 30 January 1979. *L'Osservatore Romano* 569, no. 8 (19 February 1979): 3.

59. "Address in Guadalupe to Students of the Mexican Catholic Universities," 31 January 1979. *L'Osservatore Romano* 569, no. 8 (19 February 1979): 5.

60. "Address to Workers in Monterrey, Mexico," 31 January 1979. *Origins* 8 (1979): 557–558.

61. "The Value of Music and Culture," address at the close of a concert," 8 February 1979. *L'Osservatore Romano* 570, no. 9 (26 February 1979): 8.

62. "Homily on Evangelization, Sistine Chapel," 10 February 1979. *L'Osservatore Romano* 570, no. 9 (26 February 1979): 3.

63. "Homily in St. Peter's for the Sick," 11 February 1979. *L'Osservatore Romano* 570, no. 9 (26 February 1979): 5.

64. "Evangelization," General Audience, Rome, 14 February 1979. *L'Osservatore Romano* 569, no. 8 (19 February 1979): 12.

65. "Justice," Court of the ROTA, 17 February 1979. *L'Osservatore Romano* 570, no. 9 (26 February 1979): 6.

66. "The Parish: The Presence of Christ Among Us," homily, parish of St. Gregory the Great, Magliana, Rome, 18 February 1979. *L'Osservatore Romano* 571, no. 10 (5 March 1979): 3.

67. "Evangelization," General Audience, 21 February 1979. *L'Osservatore Romano* 570, no. 9 (26 February 1979): 1.

68. "On Liberation Theology," General Audience, Rome, 21 February 1979. *Origins* 8 (1979): 600–602.

69. "Address to the Federation of Catholic Universities," Rome, 24 February 1979. *L'Osservatore Romano* 571, no. 10 (5 March 1979): 6.

70. "Movement for Life," European Congress, 26 February 1979. *L'Osservatore Romano* 571, no. 10 (5 March 1979): 8.

71. "Meaning of Penitence," General Audience, 28 February 1979. *L'Osservatore Romano* 571, no. 10 (5 March 1979): 1.

72. "The Call to Overcome Sin," homily, Penitential Service, 28 February 1979. *L'Osservatore Romano* 572, no. 11 (12 March 1979): 5.

73. "Redeemer of Man," Encyclical Letter, 4 March 1979. *Origins* 8 (1979): 627–644.

74. "Lenten Message," 1979. *L'Osservatore Romano* 571, no. 10 (5 March 1979): 2.

75. "Lenten Message," 1979. *L'Osservatore Romano* 572, no. 11 (12 March 1979): 1.

76. "Address to Military Conscripts and Their Officers." *L'Osservatore Romano* 572, no. 11 (12 March 1979): 4, 11.

77. "Humility," Angelus Message, 4 March 1979. *L'Osservatore Romano* 572, no. 11 (12 March 1979): 2.

78. "Prayer, a First on the Way to True Conversion of Heart," Gen-

eral Audience, 14 March 1979. *L'Osservatore Romano* 573, no. 12 (19 March 1979): 1–2.

79. "Evangelization," homily at the Roman parish of San Giuseppe, 18 March 1979. *L'Osservatore Romano* 574, no. 13 (26 March 1979): 6.

80. "General Audience," 21 March 1979. *L'Osservatore Romano* 574, no. 13 (26 March 1979): 1, 12.

81. "Address to the Pilgrims from Naples," 24 March 1979. *L'Osservatore Romano* 575, no. 14 (2 April 1979): 3.

82. "General Audience," 28 March 1979. *L'Osservatore Romano* 575, no. 14 (2 April 1979): 1, 12.

83. "The Relations Between Science and Faith," European Physical Society, 30 March 1979. *L'Osservatore Romano* 576, no. 15 (9 April 1979): 5, 8.

84. "Homily to the Staff of the Vatican Polyglot Printing House and of *L'Osservatore Romano*," 30 March 1979. *L'Osservatore Romano* 576, no. 15 (9 April 1979): 10.

85. "Communion and Liberation," address to members of the Communion and Liberation Movement, 31 March 1979. *L'Osservatore Romano* 576, no. 15 (9 April 1979): 6–7.

86. "Homily in San Bonaventura at Torre Spaccata," 1 April 1979. *L'Osservatore Romano* 576, no. 15 (9 April 1979): 3.

87. "Address to a Group of Genoa Workers," 2 April 1979. *L'Osservatore Romano* 576, no. 15 (9 April 1979): 4, 12.

88. "Almsdeeds: The Universal Sign of Justice and Solidarity," General Audience, 4 April 1979. *L'Osservatore Romano* 576, no. 15 (9 April 1979): 1, 12.

89. "Homily to the University Students of Rome," 5 April 1979. *L'Osservatore Romano* 578, no. 17 (23 April 1979): 8.

90. "Address to the National Union of Charitable and Welfare Institutions," 7 April 1979. *L'Osservatore Romano* 578, no. 17 (23 April 1979): 11.

91. "Address to Students, International Congress of Institute for University Cooperation," 10 April 1979. *L'Osservatore Romano* 578, no. 17 (23 April 1979): 9.

92. "Letter to All Priests on Holy Thursday," 12 April 1979. *Origins* 8 (1979): 696–704.

93. "Audience for Traffic Police," 14 April 1979. *L'Osservatore Romano* 579, no. 18 (30 April 1979): 4.

94. "Easter Message, *Urbi et Orbi*," 15 April 1979. *Origins* 8 (1979): 721–722.

95. "Easter," General Audience, 18 April 1979. *L'Osservatore Romano* 578, no. 17 (23 April 1979): 3, 11.

96. "Baptismal Catechesis in the Life of the Parish," homily at San Pancrazio, 22 April 1979. *L'Osservatore Romano* 579, no. 18 (30 April 1979): 5.

97. "Joyful Commitment of Service to Humanity Sustained Only by Power of the Eucharist," to bishops of India on *ad limina* visit, 26 April 1979. *L'Osservatore Romano* 580, no. 19 (7 May 1979): 5.

98. "Address to the National Congress of Italian Domestic Workers," 29 April 1979. *Origins* 9 (1979): 31–32.

99. "Long Live Salesian Youth," address to 30,000 young people, *L'Osservatore Romano* 582, no. 21 (21 May 1979): 3.

100. "The Work of Redemption Is Accomplished in Suffering," 22 May 1979. *L'Osservatore Romano* 586, no. 25 (18 June 1979): 4.

101. "Peace, the Church, and Poland," Polish government officials, 2 June 1979. *Origins* 9 (1979): 51–53.

102. "Homily Delivered in Warsaw's Victory Square," 2 June 1979. *Origins* 9 (1979): 55–57.

103. "Address to Youth, Wzgorze Lecha, Gniezno, Poland," 3 June 1979. *Origins* 9 (1979): 57–58.

104. "Work and Prayer: A Necessary Alliance in the Soul," homily in Poland, 6 June 1979. *Origins* 9 (1979): 71–72.

105. "The Call to Discipleship," Polish seminarians and youth, Czestochowa, Poland, 6 June 1979. *Origins* 9 (1979): 90.

106. "The Right to Work/The Right to Land," 8 June 1979. *Origins* 9 (1979): 74–75.

107. "Address Closing the Krakow Archdiocesan Synod," 8 June 1979. *Origins* 9 (1979): 92–93.

108. "Address to University Students, Skalka, Poland," 8 June 1979. *Origins* 9 (1979): 93–94.

109. "Work and Man's Dignity in Christian Perspective," homily in Poland, 9 June 1979. *Origins* 9 (1979): 76–77.

110. "Address Given at Balice Airport, Krakow," 10 June 1979. *Origins* 9 (1979): 95.

111. "For Material and Spiritual Progress of Society," address to Rotary International, 15 June 1979. *L'Osservatore Romano* 587, no. 26 (25 June 1979): 3.

112. "Children Show the Innocence Which We Must Regain," 22 July 1979. *L'Osservatore Romano* 592, no. 31 (30 June 1979): 2.

113. "Only Christ Gives Meaning to Man's Life and History," homily, 5 August 1979. *L'Osservatore Romano* 595, no. 34 (20 August 1979): 3.

114. "To the Newlyweds," General Audience, 29 August 1979. *L'Osservatore Romano* 597, no. 36 (3 September 1979): 8.

115. "Be Teachers and Witnesses of the Truth Which Comes from God," to Argentine bishops on their *ad limina* visit, 24 September 1979. *L'Osservatore Romano* 605, no. 45 (5 November 1979): 11–12.

116. "The Pope in Ireland," homily, 29 September 1979. *Origins* 9 (1979): 269–271.

117. "Address to the Irish Bishops," 30 September 1979. *Origins* 9 (1979): 320–323.

118. "Homily at the Shrine of Our Lady of Knock (Marian Devotion)," 30 September 1979. *Origins* 9 (1979): 326–328.

119. "Homily in Limerick: The Task of the Modern Generation," 1 October 1979. *Origins* 9 (1979): 324–326.

120. "Homily in Boston: The Demanding Service of Love," 1 October 1979. *Origins* 9 (1979): 267–269.

121. "Special Sensitivity Toward Those in Distress," 2 October 1979. *Origins* 9 (1979): 310–312.

122. "The Pope and Youth," homily in USA, 3 October 1979. *Origins* 9 (1979): 296.

123. "Principles of Freedom," homily in USA, 3 October 1979. *Origins* 9 (1979): 308–310.

124. "The Pope's Homily in Rural America," 4 October 1979. *Origins* 9 (1979): 293–294.

125. "An Address to the U.S. Bishops," 5 October 1979. *Origins* 9 (1979): 287–291.

126. "The Church's Unity in Love," homily in Grant Park, 5 October 1979. *Origins* 9 (1979): 292.

127. "Stand Up for Human Life," 7 October 1979. *Origins* 9 (1979): 277–280.

128. "Address to the Plenary Council for the Laity," 10 October 1979. *L'Osservatore Romano* 608, no. 47 (19 November 1979): 5.

129. "Apostolic Exhortation on Catechetics," 16 October 1979. *Origins* 9 (1979): 329–348.

130. "Apostolic Exhortation on Catechesis (*Catechesi Tradendae*)," 16 October 1979. *L'Osservatore Romano* 607, no. 46 (12 November 1979): 1–11.

131. "Papal Address to the International Theological Commission in Rome," 26 October 1979. *Origins* 9 (1979): 392–395.

132. "Memorial, Actualization, Prophecy of the History of the Covenant," 3 November 1979. *L'Osservatore Romano* 610, no. 49 (3 December 1979): 15.

133. "Address to the Plenary Session of Cardinals," 5 November 1979. *Origins* 9 (1979): 356–359.

134. "Address to the Pontifical Academy of Sciences on the 100th Anniversary of the Birth of Albert Einstein," 10 November 1979. *Origins* 9 (1979): 389–392.

135. "Homily on the Need for Unity," Church of the Holy Spirit, Istanbul, 29 November 1979. *Origins* 9 (1979): 422–424.

136. "Homily on Mary," Meryam Ana, Ephesus, 30 November 1979. *Origins* 9 (1979): 425–428.

137. "World Day of Peace Message," 18 December 1979. *Origins* 9 (1979): 457–460.

138. "Overview of Church Concerns," College of Cardinals, 22 December 1979. *Origins* 9 (1980): 498–506.

139. "A Letter to the Dutch Church," 13 January 1980. *Origins* 9 (1980): 524.

140. "Transformation of the African Continent," 2 February 1980. *Origins* 9 (1980): 573–576.

141. "Truth, the Norm of Justice," 4 February 1980. *Origins* 9 (1980): 697–700.

142. "Let Your Life Be a Song of Joy Knowing That Jesus Died for You," 1 March 1980. *L'Osservatore Romano* 624, no. 11 (17 March 1980): 4, 11.

143. "Be Witnesses of Salvific Truths," homily for Vatican employees, 27 March 1980. *L'Osservatore Romano* 628, no. 15 (14 April 1980): 11.

144. "The Moral Dimension of Study and Research," address to Congress "Univ. '80," Institute for University Cooperation, 1 April 1980. *L'Osservatore Romano* 629, no. 16 (21 April 1980): 5.

145. "Let Us Bear Witness to Christ's Resurrection," homily in Turin, 13 April 1980. *L'Osservatore Romano* 629, no. 16 (21 April 1980): 3–4.

146. "Unity of Prayer and Action the Basis of Spiritual Renewal," address to lay movements of spirituality, 18 April 1980. *L'Osservatore Romano* 631, no. 18 (5 May 1980): 5.

147. "The Irreversible Power of Redemption," homily at St. Mary's in Trastevere, 27 April 1980. *L'Osservatore Romano* 638, no. 25 (23 June 1980): 3–4.

148. "Pope's Letter to the Church in Hungary," 1 May 1980. *L'Osservatore Romano* 638, no. 25 (23 June 1980): 16–17.

149. "Fully Christian and Fully African," 3 May 1980. *Origins* 10 (1980): 4–7.

150. "Meditation on the Christian Family," homily in Zaire, 3 May 1980. *Origins* 10 (1980): 7–9.

151. "Be Mediators, Not Politicians," address to priests, Africa, 4 May 1980. *Origins* 10 (1980): 10–12.

152. "The Idols to Be Renounced," homily in Congo, 5 May 1980. *Origins* 10 (1980): 19–22.

153. "The Church in Rural Africa," 6 May 1980. *Origins* 10 (1980): 22–24.

154. "Christian Life in Africa," 7 May 1980. *Origins* 10 (1980): 26–28.

155. "The Role of the Laity in Africa," 8 May 1980. *Origins* 10 (1980): 47–48.

156. "Catechesis Continues Activity of Jesus, the Teacher," address in Kumasi, Africa, 9 May 1980. *L'Osservatore Romano* 635, no. 22 (2 June 1980): 9.

157. "Need of Apostolate of the Laity for Community of Christ's Church," homily on Pentecost, 25 May 1980. *L'Osservatore Romano* 639, no. 26 (30 June 1980): 15–16.

158. "A Visit With Working-Class People," homily in Paris, 31 May 1980. *Origins* 10 (1980): 54–58.

159. "Adequate Response to the Needs of Society Today," to leaders of lay apostolate movements, Paris, 31 May 1980. *L'Osservatore Romano* 637, no. 24 (16 June 1980): 5–6.

160. "Pope Speaks to Youth," address in France, 1 June 1980. *Origins* 10 (1980): 75–78.

161. "Reconcile Culture With Christ and Through Christ With Men," address to the Ecclesial Movement of Cultural Commitment, 14 June 1980. *L'Osservatore Romano* 640, no. 27 (7 July 1980): 16.

162. "Pope's Greeting to Cyclists," 21 June 1980. *L'Osservatore Romano* 640, no. 27 (7 July 1980): 14.

163. "I Bring You the Consolation of the Redeemer," address in Papuda Prison, Brazil, 1 July 1980. *L'Osservatore Romano* 640, no. 27 (7 July 1980): 6–7.

164. "Build Your Future on Foundation of Christ!" homily for youth at Belo Horizonte, 1 July 1980. *L'Osservatore Romano* 641, no. 28 (14 July 1980): 1–2.

165. "Who Is the Priest?" address in Brazil, 2 July 1980. *Origins* 10 (1980): 142–144.

166. "An Economy for Man, Through Man," address in Brazil, 3 July 1980. *Origins* 10 (1980): 137–140.

167. "Catechesis the Transmission of a Message of Life," homily in Porto Alegre, 5 July 1980. *L'Osservatore Romano* 643, no. 30 (28 July 1980): 4–5.

168. "Listening to the Lord," meeting with *vocationados,* 5 July 1980. *L'Osservatore Romano* 643, no. 30 (28 July 1980): 6–7.

169. "Brazil's Future: Peace or Violence?" 6 July 1980. *Origins* 10 (1980): 124–127.

170. "Communion, Participation, Evangelization," address in Brazil, 10 July 1980. *Origins* 10 (1980): 129–136.

171. "Message for Basic Christian Communities," Brazil, 10 July 1980. *Origins* 10 (1980): 140–141.

172. "The Heart a Battlefield Between Love and Lust," General Audience, 23 July 1980. *L'Osservatore Romano* 643, no. 30 (28 July 1980): 1, 12.

173. "To Pray Means Knowing the Father," homily, 27 July 1980. *L'Osservatore Romano* 647, no. 35 (1 September 1980): 5, 8.

174. "Solidarity Needed to Overcome the Problems of Drugs," homily for former drug addicts, 9 August 1980. *L'Osservatore Romano* 647, no. 35 (1 September 1980): 4.

175. "Leaders of the Next Generation Through Understanding and Love," homily for youth from Dublin, 28 August 1980. *L'Osservatore Romano* 649, no. 37 (15 September 1980): 2–3.

176. "To Contribute to Changing the World 'From Within,'" address to Secular Institutes, 28 August 1980. *L'Osservatore Romano* 651, no. 39 (29 September 1980): 4–5.

177. "The Process of Urbanization Must Be Controlled and Guided," address to Conference on Population and Urban Future, 4 September 1980. *L'Osservatore Romano* 649, no. 37 (15 September 1980): 5–6.

178. "Special Mission of the Elderly in the Life of the Human Family,"

homily, 5 September 1980. *L'Osservatore Romano* 650, no. 38 (22 September 1980): 3.

179. "The Post-Conciliar Church Needs the Laity," homily in Frascati, 8 September 1980. *L'Osservatore Romano* 651, no. 39 (29 September 1980): 2–3.

180. "An Enthusiastic Witness of Catholic Identity," address to Pontifical Council for the Laity and Committee for the Family, 22 September 1980. *L'Osservatore Romano* 654, no. 42 (20 October 1980): 8, 18, 20.

181. "The Synod on the Family Begins," homily in Rome, 26 September 1980. *Origins* 10 (1980): 257–260.

182. "The Christian Must Really Understand the Historical Reality in Which He Lives," address, 4 October 1980. *L'Osservatore Romano* 658, no. 46 (17 November 1980): 4.

183. "Keep the Faith Firm in Times of Trial," address at Galatina airport, 5 October 1980. *L'Osservatore Romano* 656, no. 44 (3 November 1980): 8.

184. "To Artisans," General Audience, 22 October 1980. *L'Osservatore Romano* 655, no. 43 (27 October 1980): 7.

185. "Social Involvement," address to the *Colloquium Romanum*, 8 November 1980. *L'Osservatore Romano* 665, no. 1 (5 January 1981): 4.

186. "Spiritual Life," address to the pilgrims of Carpi, 8 November 1980. *L'Osservatore Romano* 665, no. 1 (5 January 1981): 5.

187. "Give Back to the World the Taste for Life!" address to National Pilgrimage of French Families, 10 November 1980. *L'Osservatore Romano* 665, no. 1 (5 January 1981): 8.

188. "Energy and Humanity," address to scientists participating in study week, 14 November 1980. *L'Osservatore Romano* 667, no. 3 (19 January 1981): 16–17.

189. "Address to the Plenary Assembly of *Justitia et Pax*," Rome, 14 November 1980. *L'Osservatore Romano* 667, no. 3 (19 January 1981): 8.

190. "The Kingdom of God and the Christian Family," homily in Cologne, 15 November 1980. *L'Osservatore Romano* 659, no. 47 (24 November 1980): 1–2.

191. "Accept Sorrow Trustfully: The Lord Comes Along This Way," Angelus message to handicapped, 16 November 1980. *L'Osservatore Romano* 659, no. 47 (24 November 1980): 5.

192. "Address to Lay Church Workers," Germany, 18 November 1980. *Origins* 10 (1980): 390–394.

193. "Renewal in the Spirit," address to pilgrims, 23 November 1980. *L'Osservatore Romano* 665, no. 1 (5 January 1981): 11.

194. "Evangelization," bishops of Thailand on their *ad limina* visit, 27 November 1980. *L'Osservatore Romano* 665, no. 1 (5 January 1981): 3, 12.

195. "Address to Confederation of Family Advisory Bureaus of Christian Inspiration," 29 November 1980. *L'Osservatore Romano* 666, no. 2 (12 January 1981): 10–11.

196. "Evangelization and Concrete Holiness," address to the pilgrims from Turin, 30 November 1980. *L'Osservatore Romano* 667, no. 3 (19 January 1981): 15–16.

197. "Rich in Mercy (*Dives in Misericordia*)," 30 November 1980. *Origins* 10 (1980): 401–416. Also *L'Osservatore Romano* 661, no. 49 (9 December 1980): 9–18.

198. "Address to the Steering Committee of the World Organization of Alumni of Catholic Schools," 6 December 1980. *L'Osservatore Romano* 667, no. 3 (19 January 1981): 18.

199. "Address to Soccer Team from Pisa," 13 December 1980. *L'Osservatore Romano* 668, no. 4 (26 January 1981): 17.

200. "Address to the Boys and Girls in Catholic Action from the Diocese of Campania and Luciana (Earthquake Victims)," 20 December 1980. *L'Osservatore Romano* 669, no. 5 (2 February 1981): 14.

201. "Visit to St. James Hospital," 21 December 1980. *L'Osservatore Romano* 669, no. 5 (2 February 1981): 14.

202. "The Church in the World of the Eighties," address in Rome, 22 December 1981. *Origins* 10 (1981): 490–496.

203. "Address at the Prayer Vigil for Youth at the Annual Meeting of the Taize Community, St. Peter's Basilica," 30 December 1980. *L'Osservatore Romano* 667, no. 3 (19 January 1981): 10–11.

204. "Evangelization," homily in the Gesu, 31 December 1980. *L'Osservatore Romano* 666, no. 2 (12 January 1981): 4.

205. "The Gift of Baptism and Vocation," homily to the French seminarians, 11 January 1981. *L'Osservatore Romano* 667, no. 3 (19 January 1981): 1.

206. "Natural Family Planning and Artificial Birth Control," 15 January 1981. *Origins* 10 (1981): 526–528.

207. "Be Artisans in Implementing Teachings of Vatican Council," address to Catholic students, 16 January 1981. *L'Osservatore Romano* 671, no. 7 (16 February 1981): 9–10.

208. "Dignity of Man Lies in Christ's Call to Holiness," homily at St.

Joseph's Parish, Trinofale, 18 January 1981. *L'Osservatore Romano* 668, no. 4 (26 January 1981): 1–2.

209. "Appeal for Church Unity," 21 January 1981. *L'Osservatore Romano* 668, no. 4 (26 January 1981): 19.

210. "The Lord Becomes Light and Salvation in the Parish Community," homily during pastoral visit to Santa Galla, Garbatella, 25 January 1981. *L'Osservatore Romano* 669, no. 5 (2 February 1981): 3.

211. "Consider and Put Into Practice the Christian Vocation," homily in parish of St. Joseph Cafasso, Rome, 1 February 1981. *L'Osservatore Romano* 671, no. 7 (16 February 1981): 6–7.

212. "A Letter to the Dutch Bishops," 2 February 1981. *Origins* 10 (1981): 577–580.

213. "Salt of the Earth and Light of the World," homily to the parish of SS. Charles and Blaise, 8 February 1981. *L'Osservatore Romano* 671, no. 7 (16 February 1981): 1–2.

214. "Human Sexuality and Personhood," message to United States bishops. *L'Osservatore Romano* 671, no. 7 (16 February 1981): 5.

215. "Let the Witness of Your Faith Shine Forth in Your Professional Lives," address to professional groups and message to catechists, Philippines, 18 February 1981. *L'Osservatore Romano* 672, no. 8 (23 February 1981): 10–11.

216. "The Beatitudes: For All Ages, All Classes, All Christians," address in Manila, 18 February 1981. *Origins* 10 (1981): 615–616.

217. "The Irresistible Force of Youth," address in Philippines, 18 February 1981. *Origins* 10 (1981): 593–596.

218. "Truly Christian and Authentically Chinese," 18 February 1981. *Origins* 10 (1981): 613–614.

219. "Justice and the Land," address in Philippines, 20 February 1981. *Origins* 10 (1981): 617–619.

220. "A Message of Hope to the Asian People," 21 February 1981. *Origins* 10 (1981): 609–613.

221. "The Responsibilities of Science and Technology," address to scientists and representatives of the U.N. University, Japan, 25 February 1981. *L'Osservatore Romano* 674, no. 10 (9 March 1981): 15–17.

222. "To Be a Priest," homily in Japan, 25 February 1981. *Origins* 10 (1981): 637–639.

223. "Pope's Audience to the Jesolo Pilgrimage," 14 March 1981. *L'Osservatore Romano* 678, no. 14 (6 April 1981): 4.

224. "Always Be Close to Those Who Bear the Cross of Their Disabilities," address to the delegates of the National Association of Crippled and Disabled Persons of Work, 14 March 1981. *L'Osservatore Romano* 678, no. 14 (6 April 1981): 10.

225. "Address to Italian Catholic Union of Secondary Teachers," 16 March 1981. *L'Osservatore Romano* 679, no. 15 (13 April 1981): 8.

226. "Importance of Education Apostolate," Congregation for Catholic Education, 26 March 1981. *L'Osservatore Romano* 679, no. 15 (13 April 1981): 11–12.

227. "Be the Light of Your Community," homily at San Saba, Rome, 29 March 1981. *L'Osservatore Romano* 579, no. 15 (13 April 1981): 1–2.

228. "A Season of Preparation of Training in the Face of Future Responsibility," address to youth, 1 April 1981. *L'Osservatore Romano* 678, no. 14 (6 April 1981): 3.

229. "The Experience and Meaning of Your Freedom," address to participants in the International Congress sponsored by the Institute for University Cooperation, 14 April 1981. *L'Osservatore Romano* 681, no. 17 (27 April 1981): 1–2.

230. "Vocation of Married Couples to the Interior Truth of Love," address to the Convention on the Family and Love, 3 May 1981. *L'Osservatore Romano* 683, no. 19 (11 May 1981): 1–3.

231. "Responsibility of Charismatic Leaders in Promoting Authentic Christian Life," Fourth International Leaders' Conference of the Charismatic Renewal, 7 May 1981. *L'Osservatore Romano* 684, no. 20 (18 May 1981): 5, 10.

232. "Pontifical Council for the Family" (Motu Proprio: Familia a Deo Instituta), 14 May 1981. *Origins* 11 (1981): 63–64.

233. "The Fundamental Duty to Evangelize," message in Rome on Mission Day, 6 June 1981. *Origins* 11 (1981): 184–186.

234. "Suffering Nourishes the Grace of Redemption," address as Pope leaves Gemelli Hospital, 14 August 1981. *L'Osservatore Romano* 698, no. 34 (24 August 1981): 1.

235. "Develop to the Full the Immense Possibilities God Has Given You," address to Irish youth, Rome, 25 August 1981. *L'Osservatore Romano* 700, no. 36 (7 September 1981): 6.

236. "On Human Work," (*Laborem Exercens*), 14 September 1981. *L'Osservatore Romano* 702, no. 38 (21 September 1981): 1–13; *Origins* 11 (1981): 225–244.

237. "Movements Must Be Priestly, Prophetic, Royal," address to

Movements in the Church congress, 27 September 1981. *L'Osservatore Romano* 704, no. 40 (5 October 1981): 1.

238. "Address to a Group of Invalids from Switzerland," 29 September 1981. *L'Osservatore Romano* 704, no. 40 (5 October 1981): 12.

239. "The Path of Scientific Discovery," address to the Pontifical Academy of Sciences, 3 October 1981. *Origins* 11 (1981): 277–280.

240. "Greater Lay Participation in Life of Church," address to Fifth Plenary Assembly of the Pontifical Council for the Laity, 5 October 1981. *L'Osservatore Romano* 706, no. 42 (19 October 1981): 4.

241. "Message for World Mission Day, 1981," 18 August 1981. *L'Osservatore Romano* 699, no. 35 (31 August 1981): 1–3.

242. "Work for an Increasingly Consistent Presence in Italian Social Reality," address to meeting organized by Italian Episcopal Conference, 31 October 1981. *L'Osservatore Romano* 710, no. 46 (16 November 1981): 7–8, 10.

243. "Sustain Your Courage in the Face of Difficulties of the Times," to the bishops of Latium on their *ad limina* visit, 5 November 1981. *L'Osservatore Romano* 710, no. 46 (16 November 1981): 8, 10.

244. "Give Back to the World the Taste for Life!" address to National Pilgrimage of French Families, 10 November 1980. *L'Osservatore Romano* 665, no. 1 (5 January 1981): 8.

245. "As We Await Christ's Coming, Let Us Exercise Our Responsibility in the World," homily at St. Maria della salute, 15 November 1981. *L'Osservatore Romano* 711, no. 47 (23 November 1981): 1, 2.

246. "From Jesus the Word Incarnate, the Real Meaning of Life," Pope's address to the citizens of Todi, 22 November 1981. *L'Osservatore Romano* 712, no. 48 (30 November 1981): 9.

247. "To Defend the Inviolability of the Family," 28 November 1981. *L'Osservatore Romano* 717, no. 2 (11 January 1982): 4–5.

248. "To Make the Family a Community in Communion," to participants in congresses on the family, 7 December 1981. *L'Osservatore Romano* 718, no. 3 (18 January 1981): 5–6.

249. "Embrace With a Mother's Love Those Who Most Await It," Pope's prayer at Piazza di Spagna, 8 December 1981. *L'Osservatore Romano* 714, no. 50 (14 December 1981): 2.

250. "The Apostolic Exhortation on the Family," 15 December 1981. *Origins* 11 (1981): 437–468.

251. "The Role of the Family in the Birth of Vocations," 20 December 1981. *L'Osservatore Romano* 719, no. 4 (25 January 1982): 5.
252. "Beyond Nuclear Terror: Dialogue, 1982," World Day of Peace Message, 21 December 1981. *Origins* 11 (1982): 474–478.
253. "The Church Renews Dialogue With the World to Foster Understanding Among Men," address to the cardinals, 22 December 1981. *L'Osservatore Romano* 718, no. 3 (18 January 1982): 8–11.
254. "Let Us Recover the Truth of Christmas in Its Authenticity and Its Meaning," General Audience, 23 December 1981. *L'Osservatore Romano* 716, no. 1 (4 January 1982): 3.
255. "Irreplaceable Role of the Elderly in the Family and in Society," Angelus message, 3 January 1982. *L'Osservatore Romano* 717, no. 2 (11 January 1982): 3.
256. "To Manifest Baptism in Daily Life," 10 January 1982. *L'Osservatore Romano* 718, no. 3 (18 January 1982): 2.
257. "International Issues and the Pope," an address to diplomats accredited to the Vatican, 16 January 1982. *Origins* 11 (1982): 560–564; *L'Osservatore Romano* 719, no. 4 (25 January 1982): 1–4.
258. "Nigeria: Land of Promise and Hope," 12 February 1982. *Origins* 11 (1982): 590–592.
259. "Address to Christian Families in Onitsha, Nigeria," 13 February 1982. *L'Osservatore Romano* 722, no. 7 (15 February 1982): 4.
260. "Unity in the Church's Mission with Diversity in Apostolates or Ministries," address to laity, 14 February 1982. *L'Osservatore Romano* 723, no. 8 (22 February 1982): 6–7.
261. "To the Bishops of Nigeria," 15 February 1982. *Origins* 11 (1982): 586.
262. "The Dignity of Those Who Work," homily in Nigeria, 16 February 1982. *Origins* 11 (1982): 596.
263. "Let Everyone's Integral Advancement Accompany Your Country's Development," Libreville, Gabon, 18 February 1982. *L'Osservatore Romano* 726, no. 11 (15 March 1982): 6–8.
264. "Dignity of Work Is Part of Dignity of Man," 19 March 1982. *L'Osservatore Romano* 729, nos. 14–15 (5–12 April 1982): 9–11.
265. "You Are Precious and Irreplaceable Members of Society and the Church," 28 March 1982. *L'Osservatore Romano* 729, nos. 14–15 (5–12 April 1982): 7.

266. "Make the Church Present in All Areas of Human Activity," address to Catholic laity in Lisbon, 12 May 1982. *L'Osservatore Romano* 736, no. 22 (31 May 1982): 10, 14.
267. "Message of Mary's Maternal Love," homily in Fatima, 13 May 1982. *L'Osservatore Romano* 734, no. 20 (17 May 1982): 1, 3.
268. "Man's Future is Decided in the Family, Source of the World's Hope," homily in Braga, Portugal, 15 May 1982. *L'Osservatore Romano* 741, no. 27 (5 July 1982): 4, 5, 8.
269. "I Come at the Service of Unity in Love," homily in Westminster Cathedral, 28 May 1982. *L'Osservatore Romano* 736, no. 22 (31 May 1982): 1–3.
270. "Love in the Family Is a Guarantee for the Future of Humanity," homily in York, 31 May 1982. *L'Osservatore Romano* 737, no. 23 (7 June 1982): 9–10.
271. "The Cause of Catholic Education Is the Cause of Jesus and the Gospel," address in Glasgow, 1 June 1982. *L'Osservatore Romano* 737, no. 23 (7 June 1982): 14–15.
272. "Be Faithful in Retaining the Faith Handed Down to You by Your Fathers," homily in Glasgow, 1 June 1982. *L'Osservatore Romano* 737, no. 23 (7 June 1982): 15–17.
273. "A New Solidarity Based on Work Is Necessary," address to International Labor Organization in Geneva, 15 June 1982. *L'Osservatore Romano* 740, no. 26 (28 June 1982): 10–12, 20.

INDEX

This index should be used in conjunction with the table of contents at the front of the book and with the outline at the beginning of each chapter.

Printed in Great Britain
by Amazon

78384585R00108